T0283464

1980

1980

AMERICA'S PIVOTAL YEAR

JIM CULLEN

RUTGERS UNIVERSITY PRESS

New Brunswick, Camden, and Newark, New Jersey, and London

Library of Congress Cataloging-in-Publication Data

Names: Cullen, Jim, 1962- author.
Title: 1980 : America's pivotal year / Jim Cullen.
Other titles: Nineteen eighty
Description: New Brunswick : Rutgers University Press, 2023. | Includes
    bibliographical references and index.
Identifiers: LCCN 2022008494 | ISBN 9781978831179 (hardback) |
    ISBN 9781978831186 (epub) | ISBN 9781978831193 (pdf)
Subjects: LCSH: Popular culture—United States—History—20th century. |
    Nineteen eighties. | Mass media—United States—History—20th century. |
    United States—Politics and government—1981-1989. | United States—
    Civilization—1970- | BISAC: SOCIAL SCIENCE / Popular Culture |
    HISTORY / United States / 20th Century
Classification: LCC E161.12 C85 2023 | DDC 306.0973/0904—dc23/eng/20220516
LC record available at https://lccn.loc.gov/2022008494

*A British Cataloging-in-Publication record for this book is
available from the British Library.*

References to internet websites (URLs) were accurate at the time of writing. Neither the
author nor Rutgers University Press is responsible for URLs that may have expired or
changed since the manuscript was prepared.

♾ The paper used in this publication meets the requirements of the
American National Standard for Information Sciences—Permanence
of Paper for Printed Library Materials, ANSI Z39.48-1992.

www.rutgersuniversitypress.org

Manufactured in the United States of America

For the staff of Rutgers University Press
editorial haven

CONTENTS

1980

Introduction

Facing Janus

W E LIVE AMID multiple calendars. Some are cyclical (seasons, holidays, generations); others are linear (seconds, minutes, lifetimes); still others are personal (graduations, marriages, retirements). Within these temporal dimensions, one of the longer units of time is that of the decade. The concept of a ten-year segment as a cultural measuring stick is itself a historical construct, one that became a form of cultural shorthand back in the 1890s—"the Gay Nineties," as they were sometimes retroactively described. But such shorthand really dates back to the 1920s, perhaps because these were years in which the mass media of radio, film, and tabloid journalism came into their own, generating troves of sounds, words, and images that have been associated with particular intervals of time. Subsequent intervals have been similarly stamped and remembered ever since.

Of course, the demarcation of when decades begin and end is not precise. The twenties are commonly regarded as beginning in 1919 (in the aftermath of a world war, rioting, and a pandemic) and ending in 1929 with a stock market crash. Of course, the decade was more complicated than this, not only because so-called Roaring Twenties really only started roaring mid-decade, but also because these were years of sharp cultural bifurcation: the Jazz Age and the day of the flapper, yes, but also a time of drought, religious conservatism, and the Ku Klux Klan. The thirties, which are generally demarcated by the Great

Depression inaugurated by the stock market crash in the closing months of the twenties, are typically remembered as stretching until the Japanese attack on Pearl Harbor in (late) 1941. The "sixties" are sometimes pushed back to the fifties in terms of the Civil Rights movement and as far forward as Watergate in the early-to-mid-seventies. The twenty-first century is often regarded as starting on September 11, 2001. And so on.

The year 1980, then, is actually a bit of an anomaly in that it is widely believed to actually mark the beginning of the eighties—a decade seemingly embodied, for better or worse, by the figure of Ronald Reagan—and one globally regarded as ending in November 1989 with the fall of the Berlin Wall and with it the bipolar world of the Cold War. Here too, it is possible to quibble; there were clear signs of the economic libertarianism represented by Reagan, for example, in the decision of his predecessor, Jimmy Carter, to deregulate the trucking and airline industries in the late seventies, and the coming cultural wave of the eighties was clearly telegraphed by the release of *Star Wars* in 1977, among other cultural touchstones. But it is truly remarkable to consider the confluence of forces—conservative politics, evangelical religion, a new awareness of tradition and patriotism— and the way they were reflected in specific events, such as the "Miracle on Ice" at the 1980 Olympics, the Iran hostage crisis (which began slightly before, and ended slightly after, 1980), and of course the presidential election that resulted in a realignment, the echoes of which remain with us still. The year marked the beginning of a moment that has actually persisted for multiple decades.

This transition and its echoes have been amply documented by many historians, most recently and impressively by Rick Perlstein in his magisterial *Reaganland*, the final installment of his four-volume history of modern American conservatism.[1] What this considerably slighter book purports to do is somewhat different, in that its ambit is more cultural than political, focusing specifically on popular culture. By boring in with granular detail on a few key touchstone documents—obscure as well as legendary ones—it captures a zeitgeist as it shifts, identifying those elements that hearken back as they jostle with others that point forward. The effect will be analogous to capturing in slow motion the mysterious but unmistakable process by which a child grows.

The organization of the book is fairly straightforward. It begins with something of a prologue in the form of a chapter on the culture and politics of the year 1979 in the United States, and how that year reflected the decade that preceded it, even as there were tremors of change. It is followed by a second chapter sketching the political climate in the first half of the year, notably the early months of the presidential election campaign. The core of the book consists of four chapters—one on movies, another on music, a third on television, and a fourth on bestselling books—exploring the major cultural works of the year and the ways in which they reflected the receding and emerging trends that characterized the year. A chapter that looks at the climax of the presidential election is followed by a brief epilogue that peeks ahead to the 1980s and beyond.

For some, a book like this serves as an exercise in nostalgia. The past can be a nice place to visit, even a refuge, and I think that for many people who were alive at the time, the moment recorded here is one that echoed into the early twenty-first century—an era which, however promising or even precious it may be for any number of people, has been one of war, economic upheaval, epidemiological crisis, and political polarization. This is not the first time a large number of Americans have felt their country was going in the wrong direction— indeed, the dozen or so years preceding 1980 were one such a moment, which is why the ones that followed can seem like an interlude in retrospect.

Be that as it may, one may still legitimately ask what the larger point may be in this exercise. There are three answers to this question. The first is that readers are asked to entertain—a verb used advisedly here—the proposition that 1980 was a hinge of American history, a time when a vibrant culture emerged from a season of doubt into an Indian Summer of revival. There is an inevitable degree of subjectivity in such assessments, and indeed the same person can look at the same period differently from different vantage points in a lifespan. Which is precisely why it's worth doing—memory offers a sense of (shifting) perspective that can help us see the present more clearly no less than the past.

Second, 1980 was an important year in American history because it inaugurated an era of political logic whose impact remained the prevailing common sense long after the 1980s were over. When Bill Clinton—a Democrat elected president because he successfully repositioned the Democratic Party toward the right—famously said "The era of Big Government is over" in 1995, this child of the sixties was essentially conceding that the eighties had colonized the nineties.[2] The two George Bushes were very much the heirs of Reagan, and even Barack Obama (who had complimentary things to say about Reagan when he was running for president himself) was forced to accept the presumably libertarian character of the American economy when he bailed it out in the aftermath of the financial crisis and adopted essentially a hybrid model of health care in the Affordable Care Act. Donald Trump was in many ways Reagan's opposite in temperament when he was president, and it now appears he has destroyed the ideological foundations of political coalition that have dominated American politics for the last forty years. But the loyalty he continues to command nevertheless rests on the rhetoric and instincts of modern conservatism, even as Trump discarded many of its core components (along with the sunny temperament that made Reagan's message so appealing to so many for so long).

Finally, at perhaps the most important level, this project is less about culture, politics, or 1980 than it is a meditation on the nature of history and its role in making sense of the world. All human attempts to envision the world as it is (was, will be) are necessarily partial. That is because they are edited—their creators decide what to include, and exclude, from the literal or figurative stories they tell in an inevitable human subjectivity. Beyond that, there is also the fact that the world keeps changing, and that any truth, no matter how closely it approximates reality, is likely to lose accuracy over time. That is why we keep writing histories, and why the past keeps changing. But the elusiveness of the past does not quench the need we have for stories, or attempts to refashion them. In any event, historical accounts are never *entirely* fictitious, because, whatever their limits, they are rooted in events that really *did* happen—fixed points in time and space— even if those points can be connected in different ways, and even if there will inevitably be arguments about their shape and significance. And agreement, too, at least among some of the people some of the time. It's in the space between argument and agreement—a sweet spot that is not always obvious, but believable and perhaps useful— that characterizes the best histories of our time. The hope here is to legibly capture what amounts to a piece of slow-motion photography of 1980.

But perhaps the best metaphor to invoke at the start of this study comes from Roman mythology, specifically the god Janus, the two-faced figure who looks forward and back—the patron saint of transitions, so to speak. It would be fair to say that any given moment in history is Janus-faced, in that it simultaneously embodies what has been and will be. But certain moments seem to capture this duality with notable clarity, and 1980 appears to be one such year. The goal in the pages to follow is to bring both into focus in a way that is not so much timeless as time*ful*, showing the way that our lives are lived on the three temporal planes of past, present, and future. This is the way history gets made—and remade—all the time.

TRADITIONAL LEFTY

FIGURE 1. Senator Edward Kennedy in 1979. Kennedy was a leading figure in the Democratic party after the deaths of his brothers John in 1962 and Robert in 1968. But private scandals made his candidacy for the presidency problematic, obstacles he haltingly put aside in deciding to challenge the incumbent Jimmy Carter for the party nomination in 1980. The seriousness with which his candidacy was taken demonstrated the lingering power of liberalism as the seventies came to an end.

CHAPTER 1

On the Cusp

American Politics and Culture in 1979

SIGNS OF the *Times*:

On January 1, 1979, the lead story in the nation's newspaper of record reported that the U.S. Embassy in Tehran was recommending that dependents of employees leave Iran because of a "worsening security situation" that could endanger their safety. Another page-one story noted the striking reorientation of the people and government of Communist China away from the Soviet Union toward the United States. "America is the most advanced industrial power in the world," a university student told veteran journalist Fox Butterfield in Beijing (referred to as "Peking" in the nomenclature of the day). "We want to study America's science, its management and its political system, too." And on the op-ed page, longtime fashion reporter Bernadine Morris lamented an emerging trend she found troublingly retrogressive: a new emphasis on traditional femininity in women's couture. "Were designers so carried away by one of fashion's golden ages that they simply didn't notice how women had changed?" she asked, noting the widened shoulders and narrowed skirts that were the new order of the day. "They have succeeded in evoking an epoch in which many women, perhaps the majority, were delighted to dress as sex objects."[1]

From one angle of vision, there's something glib, even dishonest, about plucking three newspaper stories from a single date and suggesting they foreshadowed the future. It is certainly true that before 1979 was out, the ominous premonitions of the U.S. ambassador proved justified, in that Iranian students, with the blessings of its revolutionary government, took dozens of hostages later that year, many of whom were not freed for 444 days. The China story was published weeks after the government's famous Central Committee of the Communist Party Conference of December 1978, presided over by the rising Deng Xiaoping, who famously said, "It doesn't matter if a cat is black or white; as long as it catches mice"—a mini allegory of market reform that turned China into an economic colossus by century's end.[2] Meanwhile, the trend-setting, wide-shouldered look Morris noted became a signature image in the collective imagination, embodied most vividly by Joan Collins and Linda Evans in their hit TV show Dynasty (1981–1989).

But of course other stories from that day don't neatly fit into a foreshadowing narrative. There was one, for example, about how the nation's colleges were facing hard times given the prospect of declining enrollments. Yet the coming decade was generally one of prosperity in academe, fueled in part by growing numbers of women getting undergraduate degrees (they exceeded men for the first time in 1981–1982, and have done so ever since).[3] And then there were other stories of no particular significance in terms of what came before or after, like one about overheated office buildings in Chicago.[4] In this sense, one could argue, history is little more than fiction—questionable arrangements of facts juxtaposed in attempts to superimpose order on unruly sets of realities that run in multiple, and often contrary, directions.

Little more, but not nothing more: a well-wrought piece of history has a ring of truth. The attempt to craft one here begins with a set of commonplace observations, among them that growing instability in Iran, growing stability in China, and the (unexceptional) presence of female journalists on the op-ed page in the New York Times are all artifacts of the 1970s. They are not necessarily unique to the 1970s—instability in Iran has waxed and waned in the decades that preceded as well as followed the 1970s; China has enjoyed long periods of stability in the thousands of years before the 1970s; women have remained fixtures on op-ed pages of newspapers in the half-century since the 1970s. But all these developments were relatively novel at the time, and appeared to many as distinctive to their moment. That moment was understood to be longer than a day, a week, or a year, but shorter than a century or a generation. Which is why we have collectively adopted the shorthand notion of a decade as a means of demarcating time. The argument here, of course—ironically, it's a little counterintuitive given the vagaries of history—is that the 1980s, whose emerging contours will be traced in the pages that follow, really did start in 1980. Which raises the question of what made the seventies the seventies, so to speak—which is to say an explanation of not only when the seventies *ended* but also when they *began*.

This is tricky. Of course, one can say that about demarcating any decade, but scholars have been notably variegated in the way they segment the seventies. The first major book-length study, Peter Carroll's sturdy 1982 account *It Seemed Like Nothing Happened*, begins with President Richard Nixon's inauguration in 1969 and his administration's attempt to expand the long-stalemated war in Vietnam by bombing Cambodia, a move that resulted in the Kent State University protests and the deaths of four students at the hands of the National Guard in April 1970. As Carroll's title suggests, the seventies seemed like little more than an epilogue to the sixties. Christopher Strain takes this idea even further in his 2016 book *The Long Sixties: America, 1955–1973*, which expands the sixties well beyond its calendrical limits on either side, bounding it by the birth of the civil rights movement on one side and the end of the Vietnam War on the other—which effectively severs the length of both the fifties and the seventies. In *The Seventies: The Great Shift in American Culture, Society and Politics*, Bruce Schulman flips this idea on its head by arguing that far from truncated, the seventies began in 1969 and stretched through the reelection campaign of President Ronald Reagan in 1984. A similar assertion of the seventies' significance is affirmed by Edward Berkowitz, whose study is titled as a refutation of

Carroll: *Something Happened.* Some studies of the seventies have a more overtly ideological character; David Frum's 2000 study *How We Got Here* gives the decade a cheerfully neoconservative spin, while Philip Jenkins reaffirmed the general perception of liberal cultural dominance steadily giving way (regrettably in his view) to conservative ascendance in *Decade of Nightmares* in a narrative that straddles 1975 to 1986.[5]

The segmentation offered here is that the seventies was a short but highly distinct decade with a discernibly chiseled character that ran from about 1972 to 1979. The sixties was a period marked by great confidence in the efficacy of social change—and impatience when efforts of reform met resistance (hence the subtitle of Todd Gitlin's classic account of the sixties, *Years of Hope, Days of Rage*).[6] This spirit of idealistic reform giving way to growing militancy characterized the civil rights and antiwar movements, animated still further by the nascent movements second-wave feminism and gay liberation, both of which had clear roots in the sixties even as they came of age in the seventies. Reflecting this spirit of restless innovation, the sixties were also notable as a period of widespread cultural experimentation, particularly in popular music and film, both of which were infused by a new generation of artists who had an unusual degree of latitude to operate in industries marked by a state of flux (in music, a vast expansion; in movies, a sense of uncertainty among industry veterans about evolving popular taste). The spirit of the sixties culminated with a pair of liberal victories: the end of U.S. involvement the Vietnam War in 1973, coupled with Richard Nixon's resignation amid the Watergate scandal in 1974.

But these triumphs—the end of an unjust war; the constitutional reckoning imposed on a corrupt leader—were followed by a widespread sense of deflation sometimes characterized as "the age of limits." The term "deflation" is meant metaphorically (and ironically); the seventies were notable for a sustained economic downturn marked by a seemingly contradictory rise in unemployment and rising prices at the same time, a phenomenon known as stagflation. Both were inflamed by the Arab oil embargo of 1973—a year that marked the peak of real median income for men, the pain of which was masked by the growing number of women in the workforce to compensate for this relative loss in income. The ensuing energy crisis, coupled with the U.S. defeat in Vietnam, contributed to a powerful sense that national power and purpose were diminished—and that domestic reform was in retreat, notably in the realm of civil rights and in feminism, where early hopes for an Equal Rights Amendment were running into unexpected difficulty. Indeed, the year stands out enough to have merited its own cultural study: *1973 Nervous Breakdown.*[7]

The seventies were not entirely dour; many feminists and gay Americans, to cite two examples, continued to make social, economic, and political gains in public as well as private life, and there were cultural flowerings in places like Los Angeles, captured vividly in Ronald Brownstein's study of the year 1974, *Rock Me on the Water.*[8] While times were tough in the so-called Rust Belt stretching from New England through the industrial Midwest, the rise of the Sun Belt, stretching from Florida to California (abetted by central air-conditioning) was a powerful countercurrent. And there could be a bracing honesty about the state of the nation in marked contrast to what came before or later.

However, the spirit of reform in the seventies was different than it had been in the sixties. Both decades were marked by a strongly anti-authoritarian character that prized personal freedom. But while this sensibility had a strongly collective character in the sixties, it had more of a personal quality in the seventies: you couldn't necessarily change the world, but you could change yourself. The anthemic protest songs of the sixties rock bands gave way to the personal musings of seventies singer-songwriters. Hence cultural critic Tom Wolfe's famous characterization of the seventies as "The Me Decade."[9]

There was another factor at work in the seventies, one directly opposed to the permissive ethos of post-sixties liberalism while at the same time sharing its strongly individualistic and libertarian sensibility: evangelical Christianity.[10] When it first surfaced in mainstream national life in the early seventies, evangelicalism did not have an obvious political valence, as suggested by the clearly liberal character of the hit musicals *Jesus Christ Superstar* (album 1970; musical, 1971; movie 1973) and *Godspell* (musical 1971; movie 1973). By the late seventies, however, it was clear that evangelicalism, operating largely outside mainline Protestant denominations, was a largely conservative phenomenon. A new generation of evangelical leaders, edgier—and in the minds of many Americans, less reputable—than the venerable Billy Graham, who carefully sidestepped any partisan identity, now dominated the movement. Jerry Falwell, a Baptist minister from Lynchburg, Virginia, founded the Moral Majority in 1979. "It is time we come together and rise up against the tide of permissiveness and moral decay that is crushing in on our society from every side," Falwell said in a typical pronouncement from 1980.[11] Another Baptist minister, Pat Robertson, son of Democratic senator Absalom Willis Robertson of Virginia, created both *The 700 Club*, a popular religious program, and the Christian Broadcast Network (CBN) in the 1960s, both of which attained national prominence in the 1970s, thanks to the spread of cable television. So did *The Old-Time Gospel Hour* (1956–), a program sponsored by Falwell's church.

The evangelical Right was especially focused on issues of gender and sexuality, decrying what it considered permissiveness and calling for personal responsibility in individual behavior. In 1977, former beauty queen Anita Bryant reacted to the decision in Dade County, Florida, to pass legislation outlawing discrimination based on sexual orientation by founding Save the Children, an organization that worked successfully to overturn it in the name of preventing child abuse. Opposition to the "homosexual lifestyle" became a staple of evangelical rhetoric for the rest of the twentieth century.

Evangelicals were also prominent in the fight against the Equal Rights Amendment. The ERA, which sailed through Congress in 1971, needed to be ratified by 38 (or three-quarters) of the states to be enshrined in the Constitution, and there was a widespread assumption that it would do so quickly. But after a flurry of approvals in the early seventies, the push for the amendment stalled in 1977, when the total reached 35. Congress had set a March 22, 1979, deadline for ratification but voted to extend it until 1982. By this point, however, opposition had grown, led by conservative activist Phyllis Schlafly. There was also a class valence to the debate, as some working-class women were concerned about losing protections under the law on the basis of sex. By March 1979, five state legislatures had actually voted to rescind their approval, though there were legal questions about whether they could do so. It was clear, in any case, that the ERA had lost its momentum, perhaps fatally. (A number of states have voted to ratify the amendment since 2018, but such moves lack the force of law, since the bill expired, and Congress has not voted to resurrect it.)[12]

Conservatives—evangelical and otherwise—began using another tactic as well: turning the language and tactics of the civil rights movement against it. This was apparent, for example, in the mounting opposition to affirmative action, an early sixties policy designed to address centuries of discrimination by affording preferential treatment to minorities in educational and professional settings. By the late seventies, opponents to affirmative action were invoking Martin Luther King Jr.'s call to judge people not on the color of their skin but on the content of their character—in effect calling affirmative action a form of reverse racism. In *Bakke v. Board of Regents* (1978), the Supreme Court ruled that while racial quotas were unconstitutional, institutions could use race and other factors as part of a larger commitment to diversity. This compromise, tenuous at the time and in the decades that followed, reflected growing contentiousness about the impact of government intervention in race relations.

All these trends were clearly in evidence by the year 1979, when our story begins. The president of the United States was Jimmy Carter; he had been elected three years earlier precisely because he was perceived by liberals to be the anti-Nixon—"I will never lie to you," he famously said—while at the same time embracing the values of evangelical Christianity as a lifelong Baptist. As one historian observed, "He discussed his faith in deeply personal, character-based terms, combining the Protestant faith with the therapeutic turn," managing to suggest that "good Christians make good leaders" without threatening secular Americans who didn't share his faith.[13] Carter also walked the talk in his effort to reject the imperial presidency, eschewing a limousine at his inaugural, donning cardigan sweaters in the White House to conserve energy, and supervising use of the presidential tennis courts as a matter of equity. His personal decency was not in question.

And yet, by 1979, there was something dispiriting about Carter in the eyes of many Americans: he was admirable but not impressive or inspiring. This growing perception of ineffectuality intensified in July 1979 when Carter addressed the nation in his famous "Crisis of Confidence" speech to the nation. He had originally planned to deliver this address on July 5 but suddenly postponed it and held a series of meetings with thought leaders and ordinary Americans to hone his message. When he finally did deliver the speech ten days later, it had a decidedly sober tone. "The erosion of our confidence in the future is threatening to destroy the social and political fabric of America," he said. "In a nation of hard work, strong families, close-knit communities and our faith in God, too many of us now worship self-indulgence and consumption. Human identity is no longer defined by what one does, but what one owns." Initial reaction to this jeremiad was positive, but as the message sank in, more and more Americans were inclined to blame Carter for his lack of leadership than themselves for the shortcomings for which he had chided them.[14]

Carter's speech took place against a backdrop of gasoline shortages that bewildered and angered Americans. This was actually the second such scramble; the first was in the aftermath of the 1973 war between Egypt and Israel, for which the Organization of Petroleum Exporting Countries (OPEC) punished the United States by restricting their exports. This time, long lines at the pumps were alternatively attributed to rapacious oil companies, the government's reluctance to deregulate prices, and the self-fulfilling panic behavior of hoarding.[15] Such domestic economic difficulties reflected the nation's growing dependence on foreign oil, notably from Middle Eastern nations whose relations with the United States were uneasy at best (e.g., Saudi Arabia) and downright poisonous at worst (e.g., Iran, where the American-backed regime of the Shah Rezi Pahlevi was overthrown in 1979, ultimately leading to the first Islamic revolution in the modern world).

One person who was particularly aggrieved by Carter's address—soon dubbed the "Malaise Speech," though he never used the term—was his fellow Democrat, Senator Edward Kennedy of Massachusetts. After the death of his brothers John and Robert in 1963 and 1968, respectively, Ted Kennedy had become the patriarch of the dynasty and a perennial potential entrant into the presidential sweepstakes. Kennedy had considered entering the race for the Democratic nomination in 1976 against Carter, but held back because of a long shadow in his past: the death of Mary Jo Kopechne, a young woman who had been riding in the car he was driving when it plunged off a bridge late at night on the island of Chappaquiddick, off Cape Cod, in July 1969. Kennedy was never charged for his role in the incident beyond leaving the scene of accident, but his reputation had been damaged even as he continued to serve in the U.S. Senate, where he had assumed the mantle of modern liberalism. Now he began to consider challenging Carter's bid for reelection in 1980, Chappaquiddick notwithstanding.[16]

There was an opening for Kennedy to do so not simply because Carter was presiding over a lackluster economy but also because he was seen as moving too far to the right in the minds of many Democrats. When he ran for president in 1976, Carter had carefully presented himself as a man of integrity who fused a post–civil rights moral vision with the competence of the nuclear engineer he had been in the U.S. Navy. But over time his ties to liberals, always a bit tenuous, grew more so. Carter's decisions to sign the Airline Deregulation Act of 1978 and a similar bill for the trucking industry in 1980 were important indications that he was responding to an emergent libertarian strain in American political culture.

So in the eyes of some observers, Kennedy was not only an attractive prospect but a downright realistic one. That June, a *CBS News / NY Times* poll showed 52 percent of respondents favored Kennedy for president, and only 23 percent named Carter (California governor Jerry Brown, another leading liberal, got 8 percent). On July 30, the

Times magazine pronounced that "Kennedy could become president without really trying."[17] Clearly, the incumbent was in trouble. Yet Kennedy's personal baggage—besides Chappaquiddick, he had a reputation as an alcoholic and a womanizer—might still weigh him down.

In any event, there was more to life than politics in 1979. Opportunities for individuals to follow their bliss were legion, whether in the realm of physical fitness (James Fixx's *Complete Book of Running*, published two years earlier, was still going strong on the *New York Times* Bestseller List) or weight management (another 1979 bestseller was Dr. Herman Tarnower's *The Complete Scarsdale Medical Diet*, calling for high protein, low fat, and low carbohydrate consumption). For those with a more hedonistic bent, New York's Studio 54 was going strong, fueled by the hip drug of choice: cocaine.

Perhaps the purest expression of this culture of personal fulfillment was the pop music genre of disco, which blossomed in the mid-seventies. A style of music and fashion that fused Latin music, black rhythm and blues traditions, and the expressive freedom of gay club culture, disco's commercial power crested in 1979, when some of the biggest hits of the genre—Gloria Gaynor's "I Will Survive"; Chic's "Le Freak"; and Sister Sledge's "We Are Family"—dominated the *Billboard* pop chart. Disco's appeal was by this point broad enough to penetrate into other pop realms; rock star Rod Stewart had one of the biggest hits of his career with "Do Ya Think I'm Sexy," while Michael Jackson, the much beloved child star of Motown's Jackson Five, made his transition to an adult solo performer with his 1979 album *Off the Wall*, which featured major disco hits like "Don't Stop Till You Get Enough." The musical traffic went from disco to rock too: the so-called Queen of Disco, Donna Summer, was at the zenith of her power in her 1979 album *Bad Girls*, which featured the hard rock riffs of "Hot Stuff," which spent fourteen weeks on the *Billboard* pop chart and finished as the seventh most popular song of the year, right behind Gaynor's "I Will Survive." Disco's potency was evident in another way as well: the ugly backlash it provoked in the form of Disco Demolition Night, a racist, homophobic, record-burning

FIGURE 2. Donna Summer at the time of the release of her hit album *Bad Girls* in 1979. The so-called Queen of Disco finished the decade at the peak of her artistic and commercial powers, typified by huge crossover hits like "Hot Stuff" and her cover version of the 1968 song "MacArthur Park." But in 1980, Summer, an evangelical Christian, would take her music in a more traditional direction that anticipated the cultural shifts of the new decade. (Photofest)

organized by a Chicago deejay and held at Comiskey Park, home of the city's White Sox baseball franchise. It ended in a riot.

The other great musical sensation of 1979 was punk rock, which had exploded into public consciousness two years earlier with the release of *Nevermind the Bullocks Here's the Sex Pistols* two years earlier in Britain. The Sex Pistols dissolved months after the record's release, its vanguard mantle assumed by another British band, The Clash, whose 1979 album *London Calling* became a landmark. Punk rock was an American as well as a British genre, but while the Brits tended to focus on political protest, American punk had a more cheerfully anarchic quality typified by the Ramones in hits like "I Wanna Be Sedated" and "Sheena Is a Punk Rocker." The band released a live album, *It's Alive*, in 1979. By that point, however, punk rock was morphing into a related successor, commonly known as new wave, a slicker, more commercially oriented subgenre, typified by the Cars, whose second album, *Candy-O*, was released in 1979. For those who preferred their music with a little less acerbity, there was also country and western. In 1979, the genre was still dominated by assured old hands like Dolly Parton, Willie Nelson, and Charlie Pride, a rare but beloved African American presence in the genre.

Other media were not quite as vital as popular music in 1979. A decade earlier, Hollywood had entered a renaissance of sorts when studio executives, facing their own crisis of confidence, ceded an unusual level of artistic control to a younger generation of directors, resulting in a rare phenomenon: a mainstream cultural flowering.[18] But New Hollywood was also eroding by 1979. The forces that led to its destruction came from within. One was the very success of two members of its cohort, Steven Spielberg and George Lucas, who enjoyed fabulous box office success with *Jaws* (1975) and *Star Wars* (1977), respectively, movies that laid the foundations for the blockbuster mentality that has dominated Hollywood ever since, diminishing the power of directors in the process. New Hollywood was also to some degree a victim of its own hubris, as indicated by the personal and professional excesses of figures such as Martin Scorsese and the recklessness of yet another young filmmaker, Michael

Cimino, who in 1979 embarked on making *Heaven's Gate*. (More on this in chapter 3.)

There were plenty of other films in 1979 that had few of the artistic pretentions of New Hollywood but were at least as successful in terms of commercial success and emotional appeal. These included the latest installment of the James Bond franchise, *Moonraker* (starring the less than beloved Roger Moore in the title role) and the first of the *Star Trek* films based on the hit TV series that ran from 1966 to 1969. Superstar comedian Steve Martin, a regular guest on the hit TV show *Saturday Night Live*, enjoyed a novelty hit pop song in 1979 with "King Tut"—an ironic act of homage to the much-ballyhooed museum exhibit about the Egyptian pharaoh that was traveling the country at the time—and completed a pop culture trifecta of music, television, and film success with his celebrated performance in *The Jerk*. Somewhat surprisingly, the biggest box office performer of the year was also a critical favorite that commented on the fraught state of the family in a feminist age: Robert Benton's *Kramer vs. Kramer*, starring the iconic—and that's because, in keeping with the ethos of the seventies, he was *not* the classic chiseled Hollywood heartthrob— Dustin Hoffman, and the very much up and coming phenom, Meryl Streep. *Kramer vs. Kramer* won Oscars for Best Picture, Best Director, Best Actor, Best Supporting Actress, and Best Screenplay.

If the American film industry was in some ways treading water in 1979, the entertainment divisions of the television business were in a period of retrenchment. The decade had begun in a spirit of experimentation and bold social commentary with a string of situation-comedies that have since entered the network TV pantheon: *The Mary Tyler Moore Show* (1970–1977), which broke ground by focusing on an unmarried working woman; *All in the Family* (1971–1979), which openly depicted bigotry and explored touchy subjects like anti-Semitism, rape, and menopause; and *M*A*S*H* (1972–1983), a virtual allegory of the Vietnam conflict set during the Korean War of 1950–1953. For the 1978–1979 season, the latter two were still perched in the top ten, and *Mary Tyler Moore's* dramatic successor, *Lou Grant* (1977–1982), was in the middle of a solid five-year run.[19] Other seventies fixtures included the *All in the Family* spinoff *The Jeffersons* (1975–1985), about a wealthy black family in Manhattan, and working-class-themed sitcoms, such as *One Day at a Time* (1974–1985) and *Alice* (1976–1985). All these shows were still riding high at the start of the 1979–1980 season—*All in the Family* giving way to its successful sequel *Archie Bunker's Place* (1979–1983).[20]

The latter half of the decade, however, was marked by the rise of shows with a decidedly different cultural agenda. One fork in this road was unabashed nostalgia. This had been a strong cultural countercurrent to the more progressive spirit of the seventies, and was reflected in the success of oldies musical acts, such as Sha Na Na and the success of George Lucas's paean to the innocence of the Kennedy-era sixties in *American Graffiti* (1973). The Broadway musical *Grease* was a big hit when it debuted in 1972, and was followed by a smash movie version starring the rising actor John Travolta and pop star Olivia Newton-John in 1978. But the real home for nostalgia in the seventies was television, where *Happy Days* (1974–1984) and its spinoff *Laverne and Shirley* (1976–1983) served up sentimental visions of working-class Milwaukee for tens of millions of viewers each week. The effortless, if not entirely warranted, confidence of Fonzie (Henry Winkler) who appeared on both shows, became an allegory of American innocence and power with considerable appeal to audiences buffeted by cultural and geopolitical change.

The other fork in the network TV road was sexual flirtation—to the degree that network television would allow. (Cable TV, which was on the ascent in the 1970s but not yet a household fixture, would provide much broader horizons in this regard, notably in the availability of pornography.) The networks were purveying so-called tits and ass (T&A) or "Jiggle" shows, like *Three's Company* (1977–1984), featuring John Ritter as a man pretending to be gay so that his landlord wouldn't mind him sharing an apartment with two female roommates (Suzanne Somers and Joyce DeWitt). Another prominent T&A show, *Charlie's Angels* (1975–1981), about a trio of comely detectives, was also riding high in 1979, when Shelley Hack joined what proved to be a rotating cast of leads. Shows such as these superficially suggested that feminism and sexual liberation were opening new vistas of possibility for how women could live in contemporary American society, but more often than not were simply vehicles for satisfying the male gaze.

There were plenty of other diversions in 1979. In one of the greatest marketing triumphs of all time, McDonalds introduced the Happy Meal in June, which bundled a cheap but appealing toy into a package that included a burger, fries, and a drink. It sold for a dollar, a loss leader that secured the chain's supremacy for the rest of the century and beyond. The year 1979 was also notable for inaugurating the era of personal electronics with the Sony Walkman, a portable cassette player with headphones. It sold for $200—too steep for most, but its price dropped rapidly as it spread across the globe.[21]

And so it went: 1979 was a quintessential year of the seventies, really. As attention gradually turned to the upcoming presidential election, it appeared that the governing logic of the last generation—a more or less dominant commitment to greater government activism— would continue to be the order of the day. There were in fact clear signs of this.

For the Republicans, a vein of moderation had been apparent in the presidencies of Gerald Ford and even Richard Nixon, who had supported the creation of Earth Day in 1970 and the Occupational Safety and Health Administration in 1971, among other liberal measures. This moderate GOP sensibility was carried forward in the candidacy of Illinois congressman John Anderson, who entered the race in June 1979 and quickly became a favorite of college students and other voters who liked to think of themselves as thinking outside the box.

A perhaps more pragmatic alternative was furnished by George H. W. Bush, a Texan-by-way-of-Connecticut who had served in Congress as well as held appointments as U.S. ambassador to the United Nations, chairman of the Republican National Committee, and director of the Central Intelligence Agency. Bush announced his candidacy in May, but largely flew under the radar in 1979. He was noticed by political pros who were particularly impressed by his campaign manager James Baker, who had also managed President Ford's 1976 race. One early indication that Bush might really turn out to be a formidable candidate came on November 3, 1979, when he unexpectedly upended the campaign of yet another moderate, Senator Howard Baker of Tennessee, in a Maine straw poll.[22]

Even as a set of Republicans were jockeying to move the GOP from the right to the center, Ted Kennedy, after a prolonged dalliance, was finally mounting an effort to push the Democrats from the center to the left. As summer turned to fall, he stepped up his criticism of Carter, and Kennedy set up a formal announcement of his candidacy on November 7 by agreeing to a television interview with veteran CBS journalist Roger Mudd. The network cleared its schedule for a prime-time broadcast on November 4.

It did not go well. In one of the more famous gaffes in American political history, he found himself flummoxed by Mudd's seemingly simple question: "Why do you want to be president?" Kennedy was silent for an agonizingly long four seconds, and the verbiage that followed was exceptional in its vacuousness—and notable for its absence of any clear idea what he planned to do if he won. Kennedy had been beating Carter by a 2 to 1 ratio in the last Gallup poll. In an Iowa straw poll four days after this interview, Carter had taken 70 percent of the vote. Kennedy's candidacy now seemed like it was over before it began.[23]

For the moment, however, these political developments were swept into irrelevance. For it was also on November 4 that an event took place that would forever be remembered by millions of Americans as the most important thing that happened in 1979, and something that shaped the nation's political life for generations to come: the start of the Iran hostage crisis.

As we've already seen, there had been tremors at the very start of the year. Then, on February 11, the government of the Shah, or king, Rezi Pahlavi, collapsed, and three days later the U.S. embassy was overrun by demonstrators who took hostages. The new provisional government stepped in and got them released. In September, another plan for a takeover was considered, and protesters debated whether to seize Soviet or American hostages. They were dissuaded by clerics close to the provisional government, which was navigating a complex struggle for control among Islamic fundamentalists, secular-minded moderates, and Marxists, all of whom had been allied in their hatred of the Shah, who had fled into exile back in January. But now he was ill with cancer and was seeking medical treatment in the United States. Carter resisted allowing him to enter but relented under pressure on humanitarian grounds. On October 22, the Shah came to New York, igniting outrage in Iran. On November 2, college students in Tehran hatched a plan to take over the embassy. The next day, they sought the blessing of the increasingly powerful Islamic spiritual leader Ayatollah Ruhollah Khomeini, who by coincidence gave a speech denouncing the United States hours later. Mistakenly taking this as their cue, the students stormed the embassy and took sixty-six hostages on November 4 (fourteen of whom were later released).[24]

The weeks that followed were chaotic in both Washington and Tehran. The Ayatollah took a wait-and-see approach to the course of the protests, which effectively paralyzed the government even as a wave of popular support coalesced around the students. The Carter administration, in the words of one observer, "kept seeking 'reasonable' interlocutors who could make a deal, failing to realize that the new leaders in Tehran had every reason to keep the situation smoldering along." The American media, for its part, latched onto the incident with unprecedented intensity: "Never did a single story monopolize so much mass-media oxygen for so long." *Time* magazine featured the crisis on four consecutive covers in November–December.[25]

In the short run—which is to say the rest of 1979—the situation worked in Carter's favor, as the nation rallied around him, and his challengers remained largely silent. The conventional wisdom was that with the Iowa caucuses looming in January, Carter, a former farmer with a better purchase on rural America than the decidedly urban and northeastern Kennedy, was suddenly turning into a prohibitive favorite. The Republican field remained crowded, and those on its right fringe, like John Connally of Texas, looked irrelevant at best and dangerous at worst in a volatile international situation, which was about to get more volatile still.

By the end of 1979, the United States had been enmeshed in the Cold War with the Soviet Union for over thirty years. For much of that time, tensions had run high, most notably in the Cuban Missile Crisis of 1962, where the two sides went to the brink of nuclear war. In the years since then, however, there had been a largely steady ebbing of tensions, thanks to the Nuclear Test Ban Treaty signed by President Kennedy in 1963 and the Strategic Arms Limitations Talks (SALT) signed by Nixon in 1972. The two sides had engaged in a series of proxy battles straight through the seventies, notably in Angola at mid-decade. But by this point the two sides were old adversaries who could sympathize with each other's troublesome allies as much as bicker with each other. The prevailing understanding of U.S.–Soviet affairs was denoted by the French term détente: an atmosphere of easing tensions.

That all changed in December. The tripwire was the landlocked Asian nation—or perhaps one should say "nation," given its premodern tribalism—of Afghanistan. Long known as the Graveyard of Empires, this mountainous land nestled between Iran and Pakistan had bedeviled Alexander the Great, the Mongols, and the Mughal Empire before the British got enmeshed there as part of a geopolitical struggle with Russia for control of Central and South Asia known as the Great Game.[26] During the Cold War the relatively weak central government of Afghanistan managed to play the Americans and the Soviets, both of whom sponsored infrastructure projects, against each other. By the late seventies, however, U.S. foreign policy was increasingly oriented toward Pakistan and Iran, which in theory should have left the Soviets in the catbird seat. But when, in 1978, Prime Minister Mohammed Daoud Khan made moves toward closer relations with U.S. allies Egypt and Saudi Arabia, he angered Soviet premier Leonid Brezhnev, who apparently decided he was dispensable. (Both men were septuagenarians increasingly out of touch with currents in their respective countries.) When the Afghan leader was overthrown by radical Marxists, however, the Soviets were caught off guard, reluctantly giving their backing to the new regime. This reluctance was grounded in a well-founded fear that it would move too fast in trying to modernize the country, provoking the anger of rising Islamist elements the United States had been quietly aiding. When those elements sparked a series of revolts around the country, the Soviets felt they had no choice but to intervene; they invaded Afghanistan on Christmas Day, 1979.

Though perhaps it shouldn't have been, the Carter administration was shocked by the Soviet invasion of Afghanistan, the first time in the Cold War that the USSR had sent troops beyond the border of its eastern European satellites. In remarks at the White House briefing room on December 28, Carter described the action as giving rise to "the most fundamental questions pertaining to international stability," and in a New Year's Eve interview, he said, "My opinion of the Soviets has changed more in the last week than it has in the last two and a half years."[27] Indeed, Carter, who had begun his presidency in the hope of moving beyond the polarities of the Cold War, now adopted the most hardline stance toward the Soviets of any president in a generation. His shift coincided with a rising tide of patriotism and militance in the nation at large, one that had taken on a new intensity in the wake of the Iran hostage crisis. (The Senate, for its part, refused to ratify a second SALT agreement that had been negotiated earlier in the year in response to the Soviet invasion.) There was new political opportunity here, and Carter sought to take advantage of it.

He wasn't alone.

FIGURE 3. Ronald Reagan on the campaign trail in Jacksonville, Florida, in 1980. Reagan's magnetic persona contrasted with President Carter's increasingly grim one, though persistent concerns about Reagan's age and mental acuity fostered doubts that he was electable. (Mark Foley, State Archives of Florida / Wikimedia Commons)

CHAPTER 2

Wind Shear

The Political Cultures of 1980

A ND THEN THERE was Reagan.

Ronald Wilson Reagan occupied a curious niche in American life when 1980 began. For many Americans, it seemed like he had been around forever. Born in 1911 in the tiny town of Tampico, Illinois, Reagan, the son of a pious Protestant mother and an alcoholic Irish Catholic father, grew up in modest circumstances until he managed to attend nearby Eureka College, from which he graduated in 1932. After bouncing around as a radio announcer for a few years, Reagan landed a job calling Chicago Cubs games for a Des Moines radio station (translating wire reports into vivid narratives, not all of them strictly factual—a pattern of verbal embroidery that would run through his life).[1] On a spring training trip to Southern California in 1937, Reagan took a screen test for Warner Brothers Pictures and received a contract to appear in movies. Over the course of the next quarter century, he carved out a career as a second-tier actor in dozens of forgettable movies—"They didn't want them good, they wanted them Thursday," he said with typical self-effacing humor[2]—mixed in with a few memorable ones, among them *Knute Rockne, All-American* (1940) and *King's Row* (1942). It was Reagan's first wife, Jane Wyman, who was the real talent in the family; they divorced in 1948 and he married another actor, Nancy Davis, four years later.

27

After a stint in the army, most of which he spent in California making training films, Reagan began a transition away from acting toward an intensifying interest in labor politics. In the late forties and early fifties, he was the president of the Screen Actors Guild. Reagan sought to protect the economic interests of his members, but he cooperated with efforts to root out suspected Communists at the height of the Red Scare, indicative of his gradual movement from New Deal Democrat to conservative Republican.

Reagan finished out his acting career in the fifties and early sixties with television appearances, most notably as the host of *General Electric Theater*, a hit anthology series. In that capacity he began delivering speeches around the country, attracting the attention of a wealthy California business elite who saw potential in him as a champion of their values. They recruited Reagan to run for governor in 1966 against the popular Edmund "Pat" Brown (whose son Jerry would also run for president twice and eventually serve four terms as governor himself). Pat Brown became the first of many people to underestimate Reagan's appeal, as Reagan won the election and served two terms as governor. He dipped his toe in the water for the presidency in 1968 and again in 1972 before committing to a run in 1976.

In doing so, Reagan would be taking on the incumbent Gerald Ford, who had become Richard Nixon's vice president in 1973 when the elected VP, Spiro Agnew, was indicted for racketeering and forced to resign. Nixon had named Ford, the majority leader in the U.S. House of Representatives, to the post because of his squeaky-clean image. But Ford sacrificed his widespread popularity when he made a principled, if politically misguided, decision to pardon Nixon the month after he resigned in disgrace over the Watergate scandal. Ford's approval rating plunged twenty points overnight—literally.[3] It was with this hobbled reputation, and a precarious economy, that he ran for reelection.

Such weaknesses notwithstanding, was Reagan really a better alternative to Ford? Once again, the conventional wisdom was that Reagan's bid was a fool's errand. Many observers considered the avowedly hawkish Reagan a simpleton, a creature of handlers whose message was that of a two-note wonder: budget-cutting and defense spending—a pair of ideas that were at least partially at odds with each other. He was prone to assertions of dubious validity, like the one that trees cause more pollution than automobiles do, or fictions about food stamp recipients who used change from their transactions to buy vodka, or distortions like the infamous one about "welfare queens" who bilk the government of money.[4] Such sensationalizing drew widespread scorn, especially among media elites. "Sportscasting is clearly a good training for politics," an NBC reporter said of Reagan's prospective candidacy. "You learn the fine art of speaking with conviction—even when you don't know what you're taking about." Such judgments were by no means limited to presumably disinterested observers. Republican Senator Charles Percy of Illinois lamented the former governor's "simplistic thinking" in 1975, adding that a "Reagan nomination and the crushing defeat likely to follow could signal the beginning of the end of our party as an effective force in American political life." Reagan's response, given to an audience of New Hampshire voters: "You know, sometimes I think moderation should be taken in moderation." The crowd erupted in laughter.[5]

He almost, but didn't quite, have the last laugh. The Republican National Convention of 1976, which was held in Kansas City, was one of the very few in the postwar era that had any real drama in terms of its nominee. Ford went into it ahead on delegates but lacking the majority required to secure the nomination, and a mad scramble resulted, including an amusing tussle over Republican delegates in Mississippi (who, in those days, were a rare breed indeed at a time when the South was still monolithically Democratic). Ford used his powers of the incumbency to get over the top, but he went into the general election against Jimmy Carter down by thirty-three points in the polls. Remarkably, he almost closed the gap, with Carter winning a mere 50.08 percent majority. Reagan was widely criticized for not doing more to help Ford in the closing months of the campaign.[6]

Reagan was keeping his options open. Despite murmurs about his age in GOP circles—he turned sixty-nine in 1980, considered by some a little too old to handle the job of president—Reagan worked steadily to lay the foundations for another campaign in the closing years of the seventies. By the time he announced his candidacy on November 13, 1979 (months later than other candidates), his campaign machinery was already operating with notable power and presence.

Notable if you happened to be a political junkie, that is. By the beginning of 1980, most Americans were aware that Reagan was running for president, just as they had some sense of him as a national celebrity. But he was sort of background noise—a little, in fact, like Donald J. Trump thirty-six years later. Like Trump, Reagan had for decades been a major media figure. And like Trump, he was strongly associated with the values of corporate capitalism. And, also like Trump, a lot of people (still) had trouble taking him seriously: both were considered old fools who said dumb—or far worse—things, even if Trump's racism (like railing against Mexican rapists) was explicit and Reagan's relied more on inference (like kicking off his campaign in Philadelphia, Mississippi, the site of a brutal lynching in 1964). There were key differences too. Unlike Trump, Reagan's childhood circumstances were genuinely modest, and he actually had a record to run on. And then there was the very important difference in the two men's temperaments: Trump was avowedly a candidate of grievances and resentment, while Reagan projected an almost irresistible optimism and confidence in the future, evident in the speech he gave announcing his candidacy.[7] But at the end of the day, both men began their quest for the candidacy widely viewed as jokes who could be safely ignored by those who considered themselves informed and responsible adults.

And like Trump, Reagan faced a crowded field. There were eight Republicans running for president in 1980. Actually, Reagan had a fair amount of competition even on his chosen turf of the GOP's right flank. Texas governor John Connolly was exceptionally well financed, though there were early indications that he had more money than votes. Philip Crane, a longtime member of the House of Representatives and a former Reagan supporter, jumped into the fray as a leading intellectual exponent of neoconservative economics. But assuming

Reagan would prevail against this competition—and it was far from clear that he would—the fact remained that most political observers from across the spectrum had doubts that his brand of politics could prevail in the GOP. George H. W. Bush, speaking for many Republicans, famously decried Reagan's "voodoo economics," while the incumbent Carter, however unpopular, was nevertheless garnering support in the early weeks and months of the Iranian hostage crisis.

As per established custom, the first real test for the state of the race was the Iowa caucuses, which in 1980 were held on January 21. The event put a premium on organization, as the key to success involved mobilizing voters to appear in person to support their candidate. Jimmy Carter won the caucus handily for the Democrats, a sign that Ted Kennedy's campaign, foundering ever since the Roger Mudd interview, might be over before it had even really started. The real surprise—something insiders had been sensing but which now burst into open view—was George Bush's victory over Reagan on the Republican side of the race. For all the doubts surrounding him, Reagan had gone into 1980 as the presumed front-runner on the basis of name recognition alone, and his loss in Iowa did seem to be a sign, as it very often is, that the person at the front of the pack at the outset of the race wouldn't be there by the time the race was over. That had been the case with the Republican governor of Michigan, George Romney, in 1968, for example, and Democratic Senator Edmund Muskie in 1972. Now, apparently, it was Reagan's turn to founder.

The next major step in the nomination process—important in that, unlike the Iowa caucuses it was a bona fide election, and one that the Reagan team had always prioritized in any case—was the New Hampshire primary on February 26. It appears that the outcome of that contest was sealed three days earlier in an infamous candidate debate. Or, perhaps one should say, a debate about the debate. In mid-February, the Nashua *Telegraph* offered to sponsor a face-off between the two leading candidates in the polls, Bush and Reagan. But when the Federal Election Commission decided that this was, in effect, an illegal campaign contribution to the two campaigns, the paper asked each to cover the cost. The Bush campaign declined. Significantly, the Reagan campaign paid, and then invited the other candidates, without the telling Bush camp *or* the paper that Reagan had invited them. So when the rest of the field showed up, both Bush and the *Telegraph* were still operating on the assumption that this would be a two-candidate event. When Reagan tried to speak up for the rest of the field, he was told this was not permissible, and when he persisted, the moderator moved to turn Reagan's microphone off. "I am paying for this microphone!" he said indignantly (a line, perhaps not coincidentally, that mirrored one uttered by Spencer Tracy in the 1948 film *State of the Union*). Bush looked like an arrogant jerk; Reagan looked like a hero, both to his rivals and to the crowd of 2,500 spectators, who erupted in a huge ovation. It was page-one news—far more absorbing than the debate itself, which was a humdrum affair. Reagan had almost pulled even with Bush before that debate. He ended up winning the primary with more votes than all the other candidates combined.[8]

And from that point on, he never looked back. As the other contenders began dropping out and it seemed Reagan could not be stopped through the primary process, there was a brief boom for Gerald Ford, who signaled on March 1 that he could be coaxed out of retirement to save the party from itself, describing Reagan as "a very conservative Republican who can't win in a national election." On March 4, Reagan predictably finished third in Massachusetts behind Bush and John B. Anderson (who would soon bolt the GOP and run as a third-party candidate), making the Ford scenario seem more plausible. But as Reagan continued to rack up victories in the South and Illinois, Ford backed off. By the start of spring it was clear that the Republican race was essentially over.[9]

Ironically, given how strong Carter seemed when compared with the flailing Kennedy, it was now the Democratic race that would prove to be more unsettled. For all his travails, Carter had gone into the new year with some momentum. The initial outbreak of the Iran hostage crisis led the country to rally around him, as it did in his strong reaction to the Soviet invasion of Afghanistan. If Carter was having difficulties on his left flank, this was to a great degree because

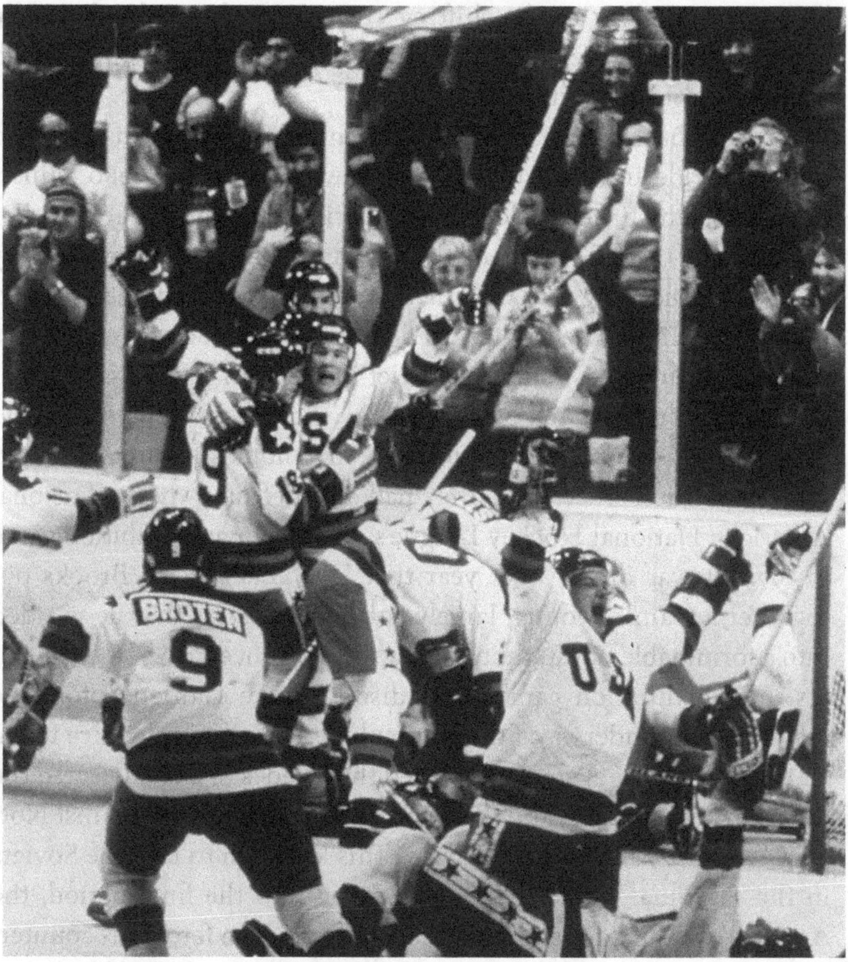

SUPERPOWER UNDERDOGS

FIGURE 4. The U.S. hockey team in a moment of triumph at the 1980 Winter Olympics in Lake Placid, New York. The team of untested amateurs bested a Soviet squad that had taken gold medals in 1964, 1968, 1972, and 1976. Team U.S.A.'s victory at a time of national trial and doubt helped ignite a new spirit of national pride that would become a hallmark of the 1980s. (Photofest) he was responding to the shifting currents on his right that were coursing through the culture at large—a major component of which was a rising tide of patriotism.

One of the most heartwarming manifestations of this surge in national pride involved the U.S. Hockey team at the 1980 Winter Olympics, which were held in Lake Placid, New York, that year. For decades, the United States and the Soviets jockeyed for prestige every four years as leading medal winners, and these winter games were no exception. (The United States would boycott the 1980 summer games in Moscow in protest over the Soviet invasion of Afghanistan.) But the Soviets pretty much owned hockey, as they had taken the gold medal in 1964, 1968, 1972, and 1976, and had not lost a game in Olympic competition since 1968. They had also defeated the professional American National Hockey League's all-stars in an exhibition game in 1979. It was during that year that U.S. coach Herb Brooks put together a team of young, largely collegiate players that he wielded into a formidable outfit, though they were trounced 10–3 by the Soviets in an exhibition game at Madison Square Garden before the Olympics got underway. Still, they cohered into an impressive team. At the Games, the Americans played the Swedes to a tie, defeated the silver-favorite Czechs, and then won a string of victories against Norway, Romania, and West Germany. This led them to face the Soviets in the semifinal round. Down 3–2 going into the final period, the Americans rallied to take a 4–3 lead and held off a ferocious counterattack to win. They then defeated the Finns to take the gold. "The so-called Miracle on Ice was more than just an Olympic upset," explained a later account on History.com. "To many Americans, it was an ideological victory in the Cold War as meaningful as the Berlin Airlift or the Apollo moon landing."[10]

President Carter, of course, was happy to bask in the reflected Olympic glory, and placed a well-publicized call to the team in the aftermath of its victory, which occurred on the cusp of Reagan's victory in New Hampshire. Indeed, coverage of the Olympics and the presidential race events bled into each other; Walter Cronkite of CBS anchored the network's newscast from Nashua on February 26, and the lead story of the evening was reported by correspondent Leslie Stahl, who was at the White House to cover Carter's reception of triumphant U.S. athletes. "What better for the president on the eve of the New Hampshire primary than to be seen on television, surrounded by a group of young, happy and victorious American heroes," she noted.

Carter was indeed about to begin a propitious run. After winning handily in Iowa and New Hampshire, he proceeded to reel off ten consecutive primary wins over the course of March, including the delegate-rich states of Florida and Illinois, giving him what appeared to be an overwhelming lead. Jerry Brown, who had run unsuccessfully against Carter in 1976 and was trying again, came in third behind Carter and Kennedy and dropped out of the race after a dismal showing in Wisconsin. Kennedy, for his part, did manage to trounce Carter in Massachusetts, but since this was Kennedy's home state it wasn't perceived as all that significant a victory. By the first day of spring a Carter–Reagan matchup seemed like a foregone conclusion. Indeed, the New York Times published a carefully balanced assessment by analyst E. J. Dionne of what appeared to be a toss-up between the two on March 23.[11]

But there were cracks beneath the surface of Carter's seeming inevitability. A Gallup poll in mid-January reported a drop in public support because of handling of the Iran hostage crisis, and the launch in early March of a new ABC news program, Nightline, hosted by veteran journalist Ted Koppel, broadcast a seemingly endless drumbeat of bad news that logged each day as the crisis continued. "ABC has finally found someone who can beat [longtime talk show host] Johnny Carson: Khomeini," the Los Angeles Times snarked. The economy—always a bellwether for any presidential candidate, especially an incumbent—was also quite poor. In the early spring of 1980, housing starts were at their lowest level in twenty years. Automakers Ford and General Motors were laying off thousands of workers. Banks raised the prime rate to 20 percent, the highest since the early years of the republic. The Carter people knew the president's standing wasn't great, but they felt fortunate in their opponents: a morally compromised

Kennedy and a Reagan they had difficulty taking seriously. "They can't quite believe their good luck," *Times* columnist James Reston reported.[12]

In April, that luck seemed to give out. Kennedy unexpectedly defeated Carter in the New York and Connecticut primaries on March 25, and while Carter took Kansas, Wisconsin, and Louisiana a week later, Kennedy bounced back to take Arizona on April 12 while ceding South Carolina the same day. Kennedy then edged out Carter in Pennsylvania, winning another big industrial state. There was perhaps less to this than met the eye; Kennedy's margins in New York and Pennsylvania were razor thin in terms of making a difference in the delegate count, and by this point the likelihood of Kennedy catching Carter was virtually impossible.[13] In an important sense, however, this was beside the point. The very fact that Carter was facing a primary challenger at all was a bad sign for his prospects, and the fact that Kennedy was still hanging on was at best a distraction at a time when Reagan was consolidating his support.

It was during this rough campaign stretch that Carter suffered what may have been the greatest setback of his presidency. On April 24, a carefully planned mission to rescue the hostages involving elite military forces was canceled after a helicopter crash in the Iranian desert. There were no hostilities, but eight servicemen died in the accident, ending what might have been a daring operation to free the hostages and raise national morale. It was one more indication of American impotence in Iran and on the world stage generally.

Carter did not, however, suffer an immediate political price, and indeed got some credit for trying. May turned out to be a good month for him politically, as he won eleven states in a row, losing only the District of Columbia to Kennedy. In June, Kennedy staged a final rally, taking five out of eight states, including the biggest electoral prize of California. But by that point Carter had the necessary 1,666 delegates to secure the nomination at the Democratic National Convention to be held in New York in August.

This created an odd situation. Kennedy had dithered about entering the race and had forfeited his early momentum with his poor performance in the Roger Mudd interview. But now that he was mathematically eliminated from winning a delegate count, he made a last-ditch effort to throw open the convention and generate a stampede in his direction. Strictly speaking, this was possible: convention rules did not bind delegates (though, ironically, Kennedy had supported rules in 1968 to make this so).[14] The summer was marked by frantic maneuvers by both sides, but Carter held the stronger position, at least among party insiders.

The problem was that his overall position continued to deteriorate in the wider body politic. Carter's brother Billy, a chronic magnet for negative publicity, was in the news because he had been hospitalized for alcoholism as well as accused of taking money from the Libyan government in exchange for promoting its interests. These stories were at best a nuisance for the president and at worst suggested political corruption touching him. They blew over, but they compromised Carter's squeaky-clean image. His main problem, though, was less a perception that he was crooked than that he was ineffectual. A July 30 Harris / ABC poll showed him with a 77 percent disapproval rating—the lowest in history, lower even than Nixon's rating at the height of Watergate. The sharks were circling. On July 31, Kennedy met with John Anderson, who since announcing his independent bid had become a darling of college students and managed to get on the ballots of all fifty states. Anderson said he would consider dropping out if Carter would as well.[15]

The more formidable challenge was further to the right. By 1980, Carter had lost significant ground with his evangelical supporters, who were disappointed that his personal convictions did not frequently translate to political mobilization—particularly with regard to the increasingly important issue of abortion—and began moving toward the Republicans. In truth, Carter had never commanded more than a minority of their support in any case, but by the end of the 1970s, the equation of "evangelical" with "Republican" was nearly complete.[16] Reagan would reap their harvest despite the fact that he was divorced and had never been an active churchgoer. But he was willing to talk their language and indicated support for their policy positions (even if in the end it all proved to be more talk than action).

Reagan, however, had his own vulnerabilities, and by mid-July, when the Republican National Convention was held in Detroit, he had his own fence-mending to do. Unlike Carter, Reagan's position going into the convention was secure in terms of procuring the nomination, though there were lingering questions about his electability.

One of the key flashpoints for the emergent right wing of the GOP concerned gender. The Reagan people successfully pushed a plan to drop party support for the Equal Rights Amendment—a staple of the party platform since 1940, and this despite the fact that 52 percent of Reagan supporters also supported the ERA. Similarly, while only 32 percent of Reagan supporters wanted a full ban on abortion, the party adopted a new plank: "We affirm our support of a constitutional amendment to restore protection of the right to life for unborn children," seeking the overturn of the 1973 Supreme Court decision *Roe v. Wade*, which granted women the right to an abortion under certain circumstances. The decision had been a growing lightning rod for Catholics and evangelicals since the nation's first Right to Life March in Washington in 1974 (an illustration of the way the 1963 March on Washington continued to shape American politics). The ERA and abortion planks were adamantly resisted by the Republican National Committee's vice-chair, Mary Crisp, who gave a fierce speech denouncing "serious internal sickness" in the GOP. Her words were met with silence.[17]

Meanwhile, the major drama of the GOP gathering focused on who Reagan's vice-presidential nominee would be, something that had not been decided, as it typically was, by the time the convention began. Bush was a serious contender, but feverish speculation erupted as stories emerged that Reagan was considering former president Gerald Ford to join the ticket as a kind of coexecutive with more of a portfolio than was customarily the case for vice presidents. The idea was to bring the two moderate and conservative wings of the party together in an unbeatable package. But the intense negotiations surrounding the idea ultimately revealed how difficult it would be to execute, and Ford finally pulled out amid chaotic, conflicting, and breathless television coverage. Losing Ford may well have been for the best as far as Reagan's prospects were concerned. As Carter's communications director, Gerald Rafshoon, later observed, having the former president as Reagan's running mate "played right into our arguments that Reagan couldn't be trusted with the presidency. If Reagan nominated Ford for vice-president, it would look as though Reagan's own party didn't think he could handle the big job without supervision, without somebody to make sure he wasn't too quick on the trigger."[18] In any event, the Republicans came out of their convention in late July united and hopeful—neither of which was the case for Democrats as they gathered in New York in mid-August.

In a way, the most remarkable thing about Ted Kennedy's candidacy in August 1980 is that he still had one. The political tides in the nation at large were clearly pulling to the right. And yet there were still serious people who believed that his brand of liberalism—one born in the New Deal some half-century earlier, coursing through the most optimistic currents of his brother Jack's successful candidacy in 1960 and the snuffed-out hopes of his brother Robert in 1968—was still a viable fork in the road. Certainly it had considerable appeal in places like San Francisco and, of course, among the enlightened elite of Cambridge, Massachusetts.

But Kennedy was a flawed vessel for liberalism. His personal conduct at Chappaquiddick and elsewhere badly weakened him among those who might otherwise have supported his candidacy. And among the old Irish working class that had been the bulwark of the Kennedy political base, there was now suspicion that his brand of liberalism was a matter of selling them out by making them bear the burden of racial integration by raising their taxes to distribute welfare benefits elsewhere. At the end of the day, there just wasn't enough good will for the party to abandon Carter: his delegates largely stood by him. And so it was that on August 13 Kennedy gave a passionate speech that became his political legacy, culminating in his famous final words: "For me, a few hours ago, this campaign came to an end. For all those whose cares have been our concerns, the work goes on, the cause endures, the hope still lives, and the dream shall never die." The following night, Carter gave a considerably more muted acceptance speech—while Kennedy's address had generated a half-hour's worth of cheering and dancing, Carter's lasted less than ten minutes. After it was over, Kennedy came to the stage, but Carter never, despite obviously trying to do so, managed to get an iconic image of the two of them literally standing side by side, hands in the air. "It's going to be difficult for the president to bring these Democrats together," Ted Koppel observed in his live coverage.[19]

And yet, for all this, with the conventions over and the presidential race now entering its climactic stage, the contest remained close. On August 20, the *Times* reported that Carter had gotten the customary bump in the polls that typically followed nominating conventions, and only trailed Reagan by a single point, 39 to 38 percent (with Anderson garnering 14 percent). This was a significant improvement over recent weeks, though many pollsters quoted in the story noted that it might not reflect Reagan's strength. Nevertheless, as former Kennedy pollster Peter Hart noted, "It's still a very open election."[20]

The times were a-changin'. The question was how much, because the winds were blowing in more than one direction. A good case study in this regard was yet another gender debate that played out against the backdrop of the presidential race: the question of women and the selective service. In January 1980, President Carter called for a revival of draft registration for both men and women amid the renewal of the Cold War. The idea received considerable support in Congress and the public at large, with 77 percent of those polled expressing approval. However, opposition was strongest among the young (who of course would be most directly affected). And support for registering women was also lower among women. For more conservative women like Phyllis Schlafly, the powerful leader of the anti-feminist advocacy organization the Eagle Forum, the idea of drafting females into the armed forces was patently ridiculous. "There is no evidence in history that a unisex army is the way to win battles or defend the country," she said. For equality-minded feminists who sought to downplay the significance of sexual difference, registration posed more of a dilemma. The easiest way to finesse it, as Eleanor Smeal (president of the National Organization for Women) did, was to oppose a draft for both men *and* women. The organization's position paper denounced the revival of the draft as racist (African Americans served disproportionately in Vietnam) and sexist. But feminist logic dictated that if men really did have to register, women must as well. According to NOW founder Betty Friedan, "There would be no basis for exempting women on the basis of sex alone."[21]

But logic was not really the order of the day. Carter's request to register women made clear that he did not intend to expose them to combat roles, an inconsistency that suggested the persistence of a belief in the necessity of recognizing sexual difference. On the other hand, even as the debate continued in the halls of Congress and on college campuses, the first women officers graduated from service academies that spring. In June, Congress passed the bill to require registration—for men only. They have been registering ever since. No woman has to this day (though the topic continues to be debated).[22]

And so it was that the wind seemed to be blowing in two different directions in the first half of 1980. It was a time when liberal ideas retained their currency, even as conservative ones were ascendant. More and more Americans were skeptical of the governing logic of the Left. And yet the alternatives seemed untried, impractical, even repugnant. All times are times of change. But in this moment, it was hard to see which way the nation was going.

ROLL PLAY

FIGURE 5. Isabelle Huppert and Kris Kristofferson in a scene from the 1980 Western *Heaven's Gate*. The cast spent weeks learning to roller-skate for such footage (much of which ended up on the cutting-room floor), typifying the excess of the production's disastrous trajectory, which ruined careers, among them that of director Michael Cimino. (Photofest)

CHAPTER 3

The Closing of Heaven's Gate

Hollywood in Transition

I T WAS THE beginning of the end. And like the beginnings of many ends, this one was marked by a satisfying victory that led to a crushing defeat.

April 9, 1979, was the day of the 51st Academy Awards in Los Angeles. A half-century into this annual ritual, Hollywood had long since codified a mythology that in many ways remains intact: the cavalcade of stars walking into the venue (in this case, the city's Dorothy Chandler Pavilion, home of the Oscars for most of the final three decades of the twentieth century); an opening segment marked by sharp humor from a famous host (Johnny Carson served in this role for the first of five consecutive years in 1979); and high-minded social-justice commentary from winning performers (Jane Fonda gave her acceptance speech in sign language to highlight the plight of handicapped people in general and the deaf in particular). Carson acknowledged the familiar liberal bent of the ceremony in humor that reflected his embodiment of Middle American values—and, perhaps, an indication of the nation's shifting ideological center of gravity. "Before we begin tonight, ladies and gentlemen," he stated in his opening monologue, "I would like to say, for the record, that I am in favor of using more Native Americans and other minorities in motion pictures [laughter],[1] I am against polluting the oceans of the world, I am for every nationality having its own homeland, I am against whacking baby seals on the head, and I am for saving the whales [applause]." He also brought on a Chinese interlocutor to make a joke in Mandarin as a mock gesture of friendship to Premier Deng Xiao Ping, in acknowledgment of renewed U.S. diplomatic ties with mainland China.[2]

The long shadow of the Vietnam War loomed in the background, now becoming an increasingly prominent topic for cinematic commentary. Fonda, daughter of the legendary Hollywood giant Henry Fonda and sister of actor Peter Fonda, had been a prominent critic of the war, going so far as to visit the enemy capital of Hanoi in 1972. She won an Oscar for her performance in the 1978 film *Coming Home*, about the plight of severely injured veterans. Her decision to take the role could be seen as an implicit form of hedging what some considered traitorous behavior, while still emphasizing the war's human cost. (Her costar, Jon Voight, won best actor for his performance in a wheelchair; he would later be a vocal supporter of Donald Trump.) The year was also notable for the release of two other Vietnam films. *Who'll Stop the Rain*, a movie with a title borrowed from a 1970 Creedence Clearwater Revival song and based on the 1974 Robert Stone novel *Dog Soldiers*, tells the story of a drug deal set against a wartime backdrop. The other, *The Boys in Company C*, took a more familiarly scabrous approach in depicting a set of clueless draftees who find themselves plunged into a cynical nightmare. "They thought the whole thing was a dirty joke," reads a line from the trailer. "You could die laughing." One Vietnam movie that was *not* released in 1978—it had been postponed five times in 1977–1978, finally appearing in 1979—was Francis Coppola's *Apocalypse Now*, a film considered at the time and ever since the definitive statement on the war as an imperialist folly (it was loosely based on Joseph Conrad's 1899 novella *Heart of Darkness*, about the Belgian colonization of the Congo).[3]

But April 9, 1979, belonged to a peer of Coppola, one he affectionately dubbed "my colleague and paisano," Michael Cimino. Cimino won Best Director that night for yet another Vietnam War movie, *The Deer Hunter*, a film that also won Best Picture, Best Screenplay (Cimino cowrote it), Best Editing, Best Sound Mixing, and Best Supporting Actor for the young Christopher Walken, at the start of an illustrious career. The night was a sweeping triumph for the forty-year-old director's second feature film. While the movie then and since has attracted some controversy—Fonda called it "a racist, Pentagon version of the war" despite the fact that she hadn't seen it[4]—*The Deer Hunter* remains a landmark film in its elegiac treatment of a working-class community shattered when its sons went to war, and one that was a critical and commercial box office success. Its ending, with the surviving lead characters singing "God Bless America," could be interpreted as having a right-wing slant, though, even if true, has more multivalent resonances than that.

On April 10, a group of executives at the United Artists corporation, mindful of what had just happened at the Oscars, met to discuss Cimino's next project.[5] It was to be a lavish, even neoclassical, Western with the title *Heaven's Gate*. Despite some misgivings, they decided to proceed. As it turned out, the project would prove to be a disaster for Cimino, United Artists, and what had been a flourishing artistic movement known as New Hollywood. Even before *Heaven's Gate* opened in November 1980, it was already clear that an era in the history of American film was over—and that Cimino's film was a big part of the reason why.

To speak of a "new" Hollywood implies, of course, that there had been an old one. And indeed there had been: it was known as "the studio system," and its heyday had essentially been the second quarter of the twentieth century.[6] In the studio system, various workers whose occupations fell into the province of filmmaking—actors, writers, directors, and technicians of various kinds, from electricians to makeup artists—were salaried employees who were assigned to work on individual movies by studio executives. Occasionally, a studio could "loan" an actor or director to a rival at a premium price, and the studio would pocket the difference between that fee and the performer's salary. While this gave executives a good deal of power over their employees, it also gave those employees a sense of financial security (at least for the term of their contracts) and, in the case of stars, a degree of pampering that came with success.

The studio system was an oligopoly consisting of Paramount, Warner Brothers, Metro-Goldwyn-Mayer (MGM), 20th Century Fox, and Radio-Keith-Orpheum (RKO) that not only made movies but also distributed them to theaters, many of which they owned. This power was augmented through a practice known as block booking, in which theaters were required to take movies they didn't particularly want as part of the price for ones they actively did. Such practices would eventually be outlawed by the U.S. Supreme Court, but until they worked their way through the legal system, a process that unfolded over the late forties and early fifties, they gave the studios a sense of power and insulation from outside competition.

Meanwhile, an even greater threat loomed: television. The new medium, which was long in coming but spread rapidly in the early 1950s, was widely perceived as providing comparable entertainment in the comfort of one's own home. That was why the studios refused to allow movies to be shown on television for many years. They tried to adapt to the new order by offering experiences that couldn't easily be replicated on TV, like 3-D movies, which never really did catch on, or big visual extravaganzas like *Ben-Hur* (1959) and *Lawrence of Arabia* (1962) that featured panoramic vistas and visually sumptuous sets. Sometimes such tactics worked; other times they failed. Eventually, the movie business made its peace with the television business as it became clear the two could be symbiotic, given that television was voracious for content and was willing to pay for old films and B movies along with recent box-office successes. Actors and other performers could cross from movies to television (though not so much the other way around); as a term of shorthand, "Hollywood" soon encompassed both.

The studio system died gradually. Actually, the death blow was not so much legal or technological as it was cultural: the old gatekeepers of Hollywood culture lost touch with a fragmenting public. Much of this was generational, an inability to tell credible stories to the newer audiences of the late twentieth century, as attested by colossal flops like *Dr. Doolittle* (1967). In a rapidly changing society, the studios also struggled to keep up with the civil rights movement, the women's movement, and the Vietnam War. Earnest efforts to grapple with civil rights, like the interracial drama *Guess Who's Coming to Dinner?* (1967), quickly became cringe-inducing in their conservatism.

The racial frontier of the new order was signaled by far more confrontational "blaxploitation" films like *Shaft* (1971), which explored African American life on more avowedly black, though still sexist, terms. Another blaxploitation picture, *Super Fly* (1972), financed by producer Sig Shore, became a hit via distribution by Warner Brothers, an indication of the fluidity in the industry. *Shaft* was directed by the famed photographer and filmmaker Gordon Parks; *Super Fly* by his son, Gordon Parks Jr., whose career was cut short by his death in a plane crash. That such movies were made at all reflected a Hollywood culture in transition in which a crisis of confidence among established filmmakers created openings for those who had new ideas with which to experiment.

It was amid this wreckage that New Hollywood began to take shape.[7] It would come to its fullest flower in the early and mid-seventies, though the first indications of a renaissance were apparent by the late sixties. A rising generation of American artists were influenced by foreign cinema, particularly the so-called French New Wave typified by the works of European directors like Robert Bresson, Jean-Luc Godard, and François Truffaut. These directors, themselves influenced by post–World War II Italian neorealists like Robert Rossellini as well as generational successors like Federico Fellini, broke accepted conventions of cinema by introducing postmodern accents via subjective points of view, informality in expression, and experiments in narrative pacing, lighting, and editing. Such influences were evident in the 1967 film *Bonnie and Clyde*, directed by Arthur Penn, in which a young Warren Beatty—himself rapidly becoming an industry force in the way he leveraged his movie idol status for control over content—starred with Faye Dunaway. The film, which featured stylized violence new to American cinema, was based on a true-life tale of criminals on the run in the 1930s. A more immediate counter-cultural sensibility saturated two other generational touchstones of the decade, *The Graduate* (1967) and *Easy Rider* (1969). The former, a quintessential document of the generation gap, starred Dustin Hoffman as a restless young college graduate reluctantly enmeshed in an affair with one of his parent's friends when he's really in love with her daughter. *Easy Rider* starred Peter Fonda and Dennis Hopper as two hippies embarked on a drug deal that takes them on a long motorcycle ride from the West Coast to New Orleans. *Easy Rider's* unexpected commercial success suggested the future possibilities for American cinema in the 1970s.

For many who lived through the decade (and many who did not) the seventies were a golden age in Hollywood precisely because the power vacuum that had opened up created the possibility for truly pathbreaking cinema. A cohort of under-forty directors—among them Coppola (an unofficial leader of sorts), Steven Spielberg, George Lucas, William Friedkin, and Martin Scorsese—took Hollywood by storm with a wave of inventive and iconoclastic films. Some of the most admired or beloved movies of the past half century, among them Friedkin's *The French Connection* (1971), Coppola's *The Godfather* (1972) and *The Godfather Part II* (1974), and Scorsese's *Taxi Driver* (1976), date from this period. Deeply personal, uncompromising in their violence, and often focusing on ambiguous protagonists, these films fused the sharp critical edge of the sixties with idiosyncratic artistic visions that eluded conventional political positions. The least heretical of these filmmakers, Spielberg and Lucas, were no less inventive, but quickly charted a path to crowd-pleasing blockbusters in the form of *Jaws* (1975) and *Star Wars* (1977). As such, they seeded the end of New Hollywood by showing studios the economic windfalls a blockbuster could produce. But in the meantime, uncertain studio executives gave such directors more leeway, financial and otherwise, than they ever had before—or would again. This was how Coppola could get away with the fiscal recklessness of *Apocalypse Now*, whose budget ballooned to what was then an eye-popping $31 million (forgivable because its early grosses were twice that) and how a promising newcomer like Cimino, who in truth was on the periphery of this crowd, could double the initial $7.5 million budget for *The Deer Hunter*, another investment that paid off handsomely, especially after it won Best Picture.[8]

No one was more aware of this situation than the executives at United Artists. The company had always occupied a somewhat singular place on the Hollywood landscape. Its founding was the stuff of legend, created in 1919 by four members of the early film aristocracy: movie stars Mary Pickford and Douglas Fairbanks, actor/director Charlie Chaplin, and director D. W. Griffith, all of whom sought more autonomy for their work and a more significant piece of the economic pie for their labors. The early decades of the company were marked by instability, and it was on the verge of ruin when it was taken over by lawyers-turned-executives Arthur Krim and Robert Benjamin in 1951, who were able to turn the outfit around. That was because, in contrast to its larger rivals, UA was not actually a studio: it had no production facilities, no chain of theaters, nor any other kinds of potentially expensive overhead that now weighed down the classic firms. Instead, it was largely a financing mechanism that cut deals with other studios to produce and distribute its pictures, which made it nimble, if always a little vulnerable. Over the course of the next two decades, UA enjoyed a string of high-profile hits before it was sold to the Transamerica Corporation, a financial services company, in 1967, a deal that reflected a broader tendency toward corporate conglomeration in the sixties (Kinney Services, which began as a New Jersey parking garage, bought Warner Brothers in 1970). United Artists remained a destination for high-profile New Hollywood directors, such as Coppola, Scorsese, and Robert Altman, as well as the wraith-like Woody Allen, all of whom prized the relatively high degree of artistic freedom they enjoyed as artists in an avowedly capitalist enterprise. But following a dispute with his Transamerica masters in 1978, Krim bolted from UA to form Orion Pictures, taking a lot of talent with him.[9]

The leadership vacuum this created at UA was filled by company president Andrew Albeck, who in turn hired a battery of executives, including Steven Bach and coproducer David Field. They were both acutely aware of the need to recruit fresh blood to demonstrate UA's vitality, not only in terms of its future success but to maintain the confidence of the stars with whom it was signing multipicture deals.

Which is why they had their eye on Michael Cimino. Cimino, who
enjoyed a successful career making commercials, entered feature
filmmaking with *Thunderbolt and Lightfoot* (1974), a deft crime caper
starring Clint Eastwood and the emerging Jeff Bridges. The film,
which was distributed by UA, had been solidly profitable.[10] By the
time Bach and Fields began meeting with Cimino in 1978 he was well
along in completing *The Deer Hunter* for Universal Pictures, about
which a positive buzz was already building. This generated pressure
with UA: while he really had little in the way of a track record,
there was also considerable potential value in getting in on the ground
floor with a talent likely to be scooped up by someone else if UA didn't
move first.

Cimino, for his part, had no shortage of ambition. The first idea he
pitched to UA was a remake of the 1949 film version of Ayn Rand's
1943 novel *The Fountainhead*, a libertarian tract. When that got a cool
reception, he followed it up by proposing a lavish Western, *The Johnson County War*, he had written years earlier. The screenplay was
based on a real-life event involving a cartel of cattlemen executing
organized reprisals—you couldn't call them vigilantes, because they
relied on government backup—against rustlers, many of them immigrants, in Wyoming in the 1890s. In some respects, the story had the
revisionist imprint of the New Hollywood generation in its plotline
involving official corruption, and in its injection of an overlooked
group of people—many of the immigrants to Johnson County came
from southeastern Europe, the descendants of whom were featured
in *The Deer Hunter*—into a familiar Hollywood genre. But the very
fact that he was working in such a genre, and wanted to make the film
on a panoramic scale (not, for example, to give it the gritty squalid
look of Robert Altman's 1971 Western *McCabe & Mrs. Miller*), suggested the underlying conservative ideology in Cimino's cinematic
vision. He wanted to shoot the movie on location in remote Montana,
and the production would include the re-creation of a period train
that would be transported to the set. It would also have a prologue to
be shot at Harvard (the university wouldn't cooperate, so the footage

is from Oxford), and an epilogue set in Newport, Rhode Island. This would broaden the story and give it more epic dimensions. Cimino's proposed budget was, like the initial estimate for *The Deer Hunter*, $7.5 million.[11]

Long before a frame was shot, there was reason to doubt this figure—and much else about the production. The head of business affairs at UA repeatedly warned Bach and Field that Cimino's budget figures were unrealistic. Cimino was obstreperous about casting decisions (though it should be said that the female lead he insisted on, Frenchwoman Isabelle Huppert, performed well in what became part of a distinguished body of work). And the logistics of the production in a remote location caused endless difficulties, not the least of which was cold, snowy weather that made it inaccessible for months at a time. But UA decided to take the plunge. After all, *Jaws* was marked by delays and cost overruns, and look what happened there. And so, while the company headed toward freefall, (screen) life went on.

New Hollywood was only one precinct in the city of dreams. As was true of other media, the film industry consisted of tiers of markets and genres dedicated to the faithful, from comedy to pornography. While *The Deer Hunter* was garnering critical plaudits and earning back its costs, the biggest grossing film of 1978 was *Superman*, part of a rediscovery of superhero movies (earlier versions based on the 1938 comic book character were released in the forties and fifties). *Superman II* would be released in 1981, followed by others into the twenty-first century, indicative of a broader tendency toward remakes and sequels that would increasingly dominate the cinematic landscape for decades to come. The trend was especially obvious in the case of *Star Wars*, which succeeded wildly beyond its commercial expectations in 1977, setting up the first of its sequels, *The Empire Strikes Back*, which would be the biggest grossing film of 1980.

Star Wars was also a landmark film—and a landmark franchise—because its general ideological outlook also prefigured the coming decade in its embrace of tradition. While New Hollywood movies were insistently subversive in challenging traditional American mythology, the *Star Wars* saga resolutely re-created a world of good guys and bad guys (along with a good princess) in what was essentially a Western in science-fiction clothing. Through a form of meta-narrative jujitsu, American audiences identified with the scrappy rebels led by Luke Skywalker against the evil empire led by Darth Vader, despite the fact that by the late twentieth century the United States was a real empire that conferred imperial benefits on citizens that included those enthusiastic moviegoers. A similar kind of transposition marked *Rocky*, the Cinderella story of an Italian working-class Philadelphia boxer starring Sylvester Stallone that won Best Picture in 1976. (The "empire" in this franchise refers to the heavy-weight champion of the world Apollo Creed, who, not coincidentally, happened to be African American.)[12] *Rocky II*, the first in a series of sequels in which the American flag, literally and figuratively, was waved often, appeared in 1979.

Rocky producers Irwin Winkler and Robert Chartoff, who sold the project to UA, were also developing another boxing film that would be released in 1980: Martin Scorsese's brutally compelling New Hollywood classic *Raging Bull*. With some trepidation, UA acquired that project as well; in effect, *Raging Bull* was the price UA paid for *Rocky II*, which would be one of the top-grossing movies of 1979; *Raging Bull* lost money upon its release in 1980.[13]

It is, nevertheless, a masterpiece. *Raging Bull* is a biopic about Jake LaMotta, the middleweight boxer of the 1940s and '50s, who, while acclaimed by fans for his celebrated ability to absorb and give punches with astounding ferocity, was hardly a household name. Frequent Scorsese collaborator Robert De Niro had shown the book to Scorsese as early as 1974, but he pushed it aside amid other distractions. It wasn't until Scorsese's bad habits during the making of *New York, New York* (1977) and *The Last Waltz* (1978) finally led to a hospitalization, and led him to reset and commit to the project.

Plot elements notwithstanding, *Raging Bull* was a quintessentially visual experience. That visual impact began with an unusual decision about how the movie was filmed: in black and white. *Raging Bull* is a film chock full of memorable images. Perhaps the most unforgettable image occurs after one of LaMotta's six celebrated fights with Sugar Ray Robinson, where we watch LaMotta endure a brutal beating, his blood spraying the crowd in slow motion. Amid the tumult as the decision is announced, the camera leaves the principal figures, slowly panning to the right along a rope so textured it seems like human flesh. The camera pauses on a patch of LaMotta's blood, which looks like a rupture in the line as it slowly drips onto the floor of the ring. While Scorsese's work as a whole eschews direct political commentary, *Raging Bull*'s fierce honesty in its portrayal of an unsympathetic yet riveting protagonist upends pieties, liberal and otherwise, in a way that seems to transcend its moment, which is why it has proven so durable.

Plenty of movies from 1980 were forgettable, but as is true of any given year there were a few, like *Raging Bull,* that have stood the test of time. Stanley Kubrick's *The Shining* is another of these. Based on the 1977 Stephen King novel, it is widely regarded as among the greatest—which, among other things, is to say scariest—horror films in the long history of the genre. While some critics (and King himself) were slow to acknowledge this, many initial skeptics did come around to appreciate its power, much of which was specifically cinematic.[14] Decades later, images of the (dead) Grady twins, an opening elevator disgorging a river of blood, and Jack Nicholson's moment of not-quite comic relief as his insane character shoves his face through a broken door and says, "Here's Johnny"—the standard opening line from Carson's talk show—have become pop culture memes. (In shooting the sequence, Kubrick, ever the cineaste, was alluding to a scene from the 1919 silent film *Broken Blossoms,* in which another alcoholic character also hacks open a door with an axe. It happens to be one of the first features distributed by UA.) *The Shining* was one of the biggest box office hits of 1980.[15]

What *The Shining* was to horror, *Airplane!* was to comedy: a summer popcorn movie that went on to become a classic in its genre. *Airplane!* was a product of the writing / directing team of David Zucker, Jim Abrams, and Jerry Zucker (aka ZAZ), who got their start in sketch comedy and wrote the minor classic *Kentucky Fried Movie*, which lampooned television commercials. While the plot and much of the dialogue of *Airplane!* were lifted directly from the 1957 film *Zero Hour*, for which ZAZ bought the rights, it was largely inspired by the so-called disaster movies that became a Hollywood subgenre in the seventies, reflecting growing doubts about the competence and integrity of official authority. The fad was kicked off in 1970 with *Airport*—followed by three sequels to which *Airplane!* clearly alluded—and included thrillers like *The Poseidon Adventure* (1972), *The Towering Inferno* (1974), and *The Swarm* (1978). Spielberg's *Jaws* also falls into the disaster category, which is marked by stories in which ordinary people confront crises, from terrorism to ecological disaster, that defy conventional solutions and in which they are largely on their own. In satirizing the seriousness with which these films made an implicit critique of society, one can discern a subtle counter-counterculture in *Airplane!*—and thus, by inference, a germinal conservatism.

The movie manifests this in multiple ways. The first is casting. The makers of *Airplane!* cleverly decided to use actors who had long histories of appearing in dramas, among them Lloyd Bridges, Robert Stack, and Leslie Nielsen, who revived his career by playing largely comic roles for decades afterward. This made the mock gravitas of these actors all the more amusing. Similarly, the filmmakers were able to procure the services of Elmer Bernstein, the famous composer and conductor who lent a similarly exaggerated seriousness in the form of musical punctuation to mock dramatic scenes. But the signal strategy of *Airplane!* is its kitchen-sink approach to comedy, a rapid-fire barrage of silliness whose cumulative effect proves difficult to resist. Some of this was a matter of pure verbal absurdity, as when the film's protagonist (Robert Hays) asks the doctor, played by Nielsen, "Surely you can't be serious?" leading him to respond, "I am serious. And don't call me Shirley." (For years to come, "Don't call me Shirley" became a joke in the culture at large.) Some of the humor was more topical, as in a scene where an older white woman intercedes in a moment of incomprehension between a white stewardess and two black passengers by explaining "I speak jive"; her character's deft use of seventies black slang is pitch perfect. And some of it relies on slapstick gags, like the truly hilarious scene where the film's female lead, a gamine Julie Hagerty, rescues an inflatable automatic pilot by giving him, by way of a visual pun, a blow job. This mix of comic strategies has allowed *Airplane!* to endure long after its many historically specific references—like a cameo appearance from antitax advocate George Jarvis, who successfully promoted Proposition 13 in California—ceased to be familiar to subsequent generations of viewers. The resolutely slapstick style of *Airplane!* implicitly satirized the notion of important social commentary as a barometer of excellence.

Other landmark comedies from 1980 have not endured quite as well. Exhibit A in this regard is the much beloved *Caddyshack*, considered by some to be one of the great sports parodies of all time (in this case, of golf). Cowritten and directed by Second City comedy alumnus Harold Ramis, *Caddyshack* posits a comic class conflict between snooty members of a metropolitan Chicago country club and the mostly young working stiffs who are both exploited and subversive (the movie featured a breakout role for the anarchic Bill Murray). But the real conflict is cultural rather than economic. This bait-and-switch becomes especially apparent in the character of Al Czervik (Rodney Dangerfield, making the transition from standup to acting), a boorish real estate baron who drives a Rolls Royce that plays "We're in the Money." Czervik repeatedly upends the condescension and hypocrisy of club members, his crass materialism lionized as a form of fearless honesty—a trope that would become familiar on the American Right in the years that followed, most memorably in Gordon Gecko's notorious "greed is good" speech in *Wall Street* (1987). *Caddyshack* featured a good deal of *Saturday Night Live* talent (Murray, Chevy Chase, and producer Doug Kenney, who died soon thereafter), but its sophomoric frat-boy humor masquerading as populism now seems less fresh than thin.

Another comedy hit from 1980, *The Blues Brothers*, was also the product of *SNL* performers, and is now similarly problematic in its cultural politics, though the overall results are more satisfying. The roots of the movie date from the opening skit of a December 1978 episode of *SNL* in which John Belushi and Dan Ackroyd rendered a cover version of the 1967 Sam and Dave hit "Soul Man," accompanied by a crack backing band whose members played on any number of great soul hits from that era. Belushi and Ackroyd's rendition of the song would go on to become a pop hit. Ackroyd subsequently produced a sprawling script for a movie that was directed by John Landis (of *Animal House* fame, written by Ramis and Kenney) featuring a broad array of musical legends that included Cab Calloway, Ray Charles, James Brown and Aretha Franklin, who also happened to turn in a nice bit of acting. Today *The Blues Brothers* would be regarded by some as a long exercise in cultural appropriation, given that Belushi and Ackroyd enjoyed more screen time than their musical talent would suggest, and reaped a disproportionate share of the attention and financial reward. But the quality of the performances and the film's valentine to working-class Chicago at least partially redeems such excesses, sustaining the memory of great African American music for another generation.

One African American artist of 1980 who did get the prominence he deserved was Richard Pryor, who costarred with Gene Wilder in the second and most successful of their five-film collaboration in *Stir Crazy*, directed by Sidney Poitier, the acting legend who moved behind the camera for this effort. Pryor and Wilder play two hapless drifters who get framed for a bank robbery and sent to jail, where they plot an escape rooted in the ability of Wilder's character to ride a mechanical bull (something of a fad in light of the success of *Urban Cowboy*, yet to be discussed). *Stir Crazy* is only mildly amusing, and its production was hobbled by Pryor's drug addiction, a problem that also afflicted Belushi and similarly hampered *The Blues Brothers*. Here, Pryor is simply not the incandescent performer who electrified audiences in his standup act. He nevertheless remained a deeply compelling presence, and *Stir Crazy* was the second most successful film of 1980 at the box office after *The Empire Strikes Back*.[16]

The year also had its share of dramatic films. Actually, one of the most financially successful was also a prison story: *Brubaker*, starring

Robert Redford as the real-life reformer Henry Brubaker, warden of the Wakefield State Prison in Arkansas during the sixties. The movie adds an undercover plot element in which Brubaker lives among the inmates to document their conditions, but the real-life character's efforts did result in a 1970 federal court case that ruled that the state's prison system violated inmates' constitutional rights, which led to reforms. "Although admittedly Wakefield is an imperfect institution, much like America herself, she is nevertheless a grand experiment— government of the man, for the man, by the man," a state senator tells Brubaker toward the end of the film. His unwitting use of "the man"—leftist shorthand for "white power structure"—undermines his credibility. He then completes his unwitting damnation: "Plus the fact that it is the only prison in the United States that's shown a profit." Naturally, Redford's character shows such logic to be bankrupt.

For many years Redford had been the quintessential Hollywood movie star with predictably liberal values, but 1980 was also the year in which he made his directorial debut with *Ordinary People*, an auspicious beginning, as he won Best Director and the film took the Best Picture at the 1981 Oscar ceremonies. A family drama based on the 1976 novel by Judith Guest, *Ordinary People* starred Donald Sutherland and Mary Tyler Moore as grief-stricken parents who lost their elder son in a boating accident that also involved their younger son (Timothy Hutton), who survived and is haunted by the experience. In a film chock-full of fine performances, it was Moore's which stood out, because as the former star of *The Dick Van Dyke Show* (1961–1966) and the *Mary Tyler Moore Show* (1970–1977) she was cast against type as a chilly, passive-aggressive mother. There's something almost too tasteful about the movie, whose middlebrow sensibility seems in such sharp contrast to its Oscar competitor *Raging Bull*, which is obviously a tour-de-force of filmmaking. (One telling indication of this is *Ordinary People*'s use of Pachelbel's Canon, a previously obscure piece of classical music whose prominence soared after the film's release.)[17] But *Ordinary People* is, among other things, a remarkable social document of bourgeois life on the cusp of the eighties, and its depiction of suburban Chicago seems downright lush—and undoubtedly out of reach now for all but the wealthiest of American families. While the family's affluence is meant to serve as a foil for its psychic misery, it is also nevertheless suggestive of a materialism that would become notably more prominent in the eighties.

There were also some good portrayals of working-class life in 1980. One of the best was retrospective: British director Michael Apted's biopic of Loretta Lynn, *Coal Miner's Daughter*, which starred Sissy Spacek in an Oscar-winning turn as the country music star in which she actually performs Lynn's songs herself. Apted, a versatile director whose credits would run from James Bond to a celebrated series of documentaries tracing the lives of a group of ordinary British citizens as they aged (all the way from *7 Up* in 1964 to *63 Up* in 2019 before his death in 2021), showed unusual sensitivity in capturing the lives of the characters in the story, aided by Tom Rickman's screenplay and a very strong cast that included Tommy Lee Jones, Levon Helm, and Beverly D'Angelo as Lynn's pal Patsy Cline. The film traced Lynn's hardscrabble roots in rural Kentucky to her superstardom in ways that documented her grit as well as her talent.

While it was hardly a sociological treatise, another compelling rendition of working-class life in 1980—one indicative of a larger shift in American society away from the Rust Belt to the Sun Belt—was *Urban Cowboy*, which also did well at the summer box office and whose soundtrack spawned a series of hits. The movie, directed by veteran hitmaker James Bridges, was based on a 1978 article in *Esquire* magazine by Aaron Latham, who was sent to the Houston suburb of Pasadena by celebrated editor Clay Felker to document the scene at Gilley's, a country music nightclub that attracted petroleum workers during the late seventies oil boom. (We see plenty of pickup trucks in the parking lot, and pickup couples in the barroom.) *Urban Cowboy* depicts a fairly traditional love triangle between characters played by Scott Glenn, Debra Winger, and John Travolta, a superstar who had gone a bit cold with his 1979 film *Moment to Moment* and was looking to get back in the saddle again. This he did literally in *Urban Cowboy*, since the story featured the mechanical bulls that were a big fad at the time. While the movie had more than its fair share of glitz and star power, its opening sequence in particular does a fine job of capturing the industrial landscape of late twentieth-century Houston. In the context of that moment, country music culture, with its strongly conservative tendencies, seemed to some a more realistic and authentic expression of national identity than the faddish worlds of punk, disco, and other subcultures. The subhead of Latham's *Esquire* piece captured the ethos of the subsequent movie: "In these anxious times, some Americans have turned to God; others, to gurus. But more and more turn to the cowboy hat."[18] The line was also indicative of a coming return to traditional masculinity.

A more cartoonish, but immensely profitable, depiction of Texas life was *Smokey and the Bandit II*, the 1980 sequel to the 1977 road chase movie, which was made on a shoestring budget of $4.3 million and ended up grossing almost thirty times that. The "Smokey" in question was Burt Reynolds, the biggest movie star in the world at the time, starring in a road movie involving the illegal transportation of Coors beer—back then considered a rare working-class delicacy—across state lines. The 1980 sequel was basically the same story, but the contraband in question this time was an elephant to be delivered to the Republican National Convention. *Smokey II* also finished in the top ten grossing movies of the year.[19]

Though it was otherwise forgettable, one movie that captured another specific socioeconomic moment in 1980 was *How to Beat the High Cost of Living*, starring Susan Saint James, Jessica Lange, and *SNL* star Jane Curtin as three middle-aged high school friends in suburban Oregon besieged by the very real inflationary pressures in the economy. ("It's not us, it's the Arabs," a gas station attendant tells Curtin's character when she laments a 9-cent rise in a gallon of gas from the previous week.) The women decide to take matters into their own hands by robbing a local mall. Their caper, like the strip tease that Curtin's character performs as a distraction in the process of their executing the robbery, comes off as a bit lame. But the film does capture the struggles of middle-class women who can no longer depend on the men in their lives for their economic well-being, whether because they are divorced or because current or former husbands are less willing or able to shoulder breadwinning responsibilities.

This sense of shifting family and gender tides—and the limits of the alternative arrangements that followed in their wake—is apparent in another minor comedy, *Serial,* based on the episodic 1977 novel by Cynthia McFadden. The movie stars Martin Mull as what we understand to be a fairly normal man in fairly abnormal Marin County, California, where alternative lifestyles are the norm. Roger Ebert's review at the time captures its essence: "These creatures ride bicycles to the ferry to conserve fuel. They are all going to the shrink. They trade spouses. Their kids join obscure religious cults. Their hearts are filled with love, their minds with dread, their bowels with bran. Their marriages and memorial services are holdovers from the days of the flower children, with incantations about the earth and the sky and doing your own thing."[20] The key to the film—the trait that marks it as a document of a transitional time—is the snarky stance it takes toward its material. "These are exciting times, aren't they? Gas is over a dollar and it's okay to be an asshole," Mull's character says of the period's tendency to conflate wisdom and self-fulfillment.

Other films from the period are less satirical about shifting social mores but are caught between looking backward and moving forward at the same time. One very good example of this, worth exploring in some detail, is another small movie by a big-time Hollywood heavyweight. In January 1980, Warner Brothers released *Just Tell Me What You Want*—whose provocative script was written by Jay Presson Allen, a veteran screenwriter and one of the few women of the time to earn such a credit. The film, like a number of Allen projects, was directed by Sidney Lumet, a highly regarded director whose track record— distinguished by prior successes such as *Serpico* (1973), *Dog Day Afternoon* (1975), and *Network* (1976)—made him one of the most admired filmmakers of his time. He went on to score hits with *Prince of the City* (1981) and *The Verdict* (1982), and by the time of his death in 2011 he was regarded as a major artist, as well as the author of *Making*

Movies, a classic book on filmmaking. But *Just Tell Me What You Want* was a flop. It is a measure of Lumet's stature that it was made in the first place, and even more so that his career survived its box office failure (the film finished at #111 at the box office).[21]

It is, nevertheless, a revealing document. *Just Tell Me What You Want* stars Ali McGraw, the iconic movie star whose performance in *Love Story* (1970) was a touchstone document of the sixties. Here she plays Bones Burton, the longtime mistress of Max Herschel (Alan King), a corporate baron. As her unusual name suggests, Bones is a tough-minded feminist who herself is a successful businesswoman. She wants to take over a movie studio that Max has just bought in order to break it up and sell off its components (a practice that would become standard operating procedure for Wall Street raiders such as Michael Milken and Carl Icahn in the eighties). Early in the film, we learn that Max has just paid for—another—abortion for Bones, a plot point notable for its off-handed treatment. *Roe v. Wade* had made abortion legal in the years before the film was made, and abortion rights were well on their way to becoming prevailing common sense among liberals in these years. But the issue was nevertheless deeply controversial amid the evangelicals ascendant in 1980—and, more to the point, would become more so in the coming years. In decades to come the subject would be avoided entirely in mainstream Hollywood movies, and to the extent it was engaged, it would be with a gravity notably lacking *Just Tell Me What You Want* (and usually ending with the woman in question deciding to keep the baby). Bones's offhand feminism is apparent in the sexual emancipation she wears lightly—when Max denies her what she wants she takes up with another man—and the amusing physical beating she administers to Max at Bergdorf Goodman, a swanky Fifth Avenue department store. (It draws an approving crowd.) In these ways, then, *Just Tell Me What You Want* is a movie of the 1970s.

In others, however, it bears the unmistakable fingerprints of the coming eighties. This is most obvious in its evident—and, given the larger context, shockingly—unapologetic embrace of finance capitalism. In the prevailing logic of the time (perhaps any time),

Max Herschel should be a monster: an amoral, grasping plutocrat. But we're meant to like him—he's funny, devoted in his way to his mentally impaired wife, and shrewd in grasping the limits of Bones's new novelist / screenwriter husband. He proves to be a worthy match for Bones, a man who will absorb abuse in the name of love. What may be most remarkable of all about this story, though, is that it is cinematically rendered by Sidney Lumet, of all people, a director with a long-established record as a liberal lion in films that have explored police corruption, homosexuality, and nuclear war. While *Just Tell Me What You Want* was a commercial bust—and, in truth, it is not a very good movie, even though its craftsmanship is evident—the film does suggest the way the sharpest minds of the country nevertheless had a finger in the wind as to which way the culture was blowing.

One movie that is both a little dated and ahead of its time was among the biggest hits of 1980, *9 to 5*. The film stars three feminist icons: Jane Fonda, Lily Tomlin, and Dolly Parton. Parton also wrote and performed the marvelous chart-topping theme song whose percussive rhythm is accented by typewriters. The three play support staff working for a boorish Dabney Coleman in the kind of part he made a specialty in his half-century-long career. Naturally, sisterhood is powerful, and the three very different women—the mousy Fonda, ingenuous Parton, and more assertive Tomlin—team up to give him his just desserts, which culminate with his corporate chieftain boss agreeing to notably forward-looking demands from the women that include child care, part-time work, and flex time. Notably missing here is equal pay; even fantasies have limits.

Perhaps no one was more attuned to the cross-currents of the decade's transition than Goldie Hawn. Hawn—who began her career as a sexpot on the TV sketch comedy *Rowan & Martin's Laugh-In* in 1968, and went on to movie stardom in the seventies before becoming a performer / impresario in the decades that followed—had a very good year in 1980. That was because she had two hit movies. The first, which she coproduced, and whose script was written with her in mind, was *Private Benjamin*, which finished seventh at the box office.[22]

MILITARY OUTFIT

FIGURE 6. Goldie Hawn in *Private Benjamin*. A fish-out-of-water tale in which a Jewish-American Princess finds herself in the U.S. Army, the 1980 film cannily blends seventies-style feminism with a newly positive stance toward military life in the wake of caustic cinematic Vietnam critiques. (Photofest)

Private Benjamin is a very canny movie. A fish-out-of-water tale in which a Jewish-American Princess finds herself in the U.S. Army, it achieves impressive comic effect because of the way it works both ends of that equation. Even before we meet Hawn's character, Judith Benjamin, a title card tells us that all the woman we're about meet has ever wanted is a big house with "nice clothes, two closets, and a professional man as a husband." In the opening scene her dream comes true with her marriage to lawyer Yale Goodman (Albert Brooks), even if the upholstery on the ottoman she has received as a wedding gift isn't quite up to snuff. But Judy's life of bliss is ruptured on her wedding night when Yale dies suddenly of a heart attack in the heat of coitus. Bereft and suffocated by the concerns of family and friends, Judy makes an impulsive decision to join the army, one for which she is woefully unprepared—"Is green the only color?" she asks of her fatigues—and which she cannot easily undo. But because she's so obviously in over her head ("I've never met as whiny a candy-ass as you," her training officer, played by veteran character Eileen Brennan, observes), a discharge from Fort Biloxi is arranged. The arrival of her parents steels something in Private Benjamin, however, who, naturally, learns the ropes and becomes an effective soldier. Along the way she meets a charming French doctor who sweeps her off her feet but who proves to be a cad. The movie comes full circle to end with a wedding, but this time Judy slugs the groom, rips off her tiara, and walks off to make her own way in the world. A story whose trajectory you can see a mile away—an inverted Cinderella tale for the post-feminist world in which the story is set—it is no less satisfying for that. Much of the reason rests in Hawn's undeniable charisma.

However, *Private Benjamin* also deploys military tropes alongside the feminist ones, and these are the more intriguing ones. The movie's poster, which shows an immiserated Hawn wearing an army helmet in the rain, is clearly modeled on a similar image from the 1930 movie version of *All Quiet on the Western Front*. Judy's squad, which consists of her aristocratic Jewish Philly self, a black woman, an urban convict, and a Southern good-ole-gal, mimics that of countless World War II movies in which a diverse and bickering team must and does come together to achieve victory. Judy's success as a soldier is a matter of good basic training, but also more than a dollop of American ingenuity that relies on tactics that go beyond anything in the rule book. And when she's sexually assaulted by her commanding officer, she turns the tables and parlays his fear of exposure into a promotion. Metanarratively speaking, we've seen this movie (and never get tired of watching it).

But in the context of 1980, the most notable thing about *Private Benjamin* is that it is a mainstream American comedy about the armed forces. Now *that* is novel. In the seventies, military stories had been epic dramas like *Patton* (1970), more often than not focusing on American failures, ranging from *A Bridge Too Far* (1977) to *Apocalypse Now* at decade's end. *Private Benjamin* is not only a comedy but one that affirms a soldier's life, in that it makes a woman out of Judy. As such, it was the first of a series of eighties movies that includes *Stripes* (1981), *An Officer and a Gentleman* (1982), and *Biloxi Blues* (1988) that portray the military in a comic or positive light with none of the savage satire of a movie like *Dr. Strangelove* (1964) or *The Boys from Company C*. This suggests a neoconservative air to such movies, even when, as in the case of *Private Benjamin*, there is little doubt of the filmmakers' core liberal sympathies.

The aforementioned *Biloxi Blues* was based on the 1985 play by Neil Simon, who became a one-man cottage industry of Tony and Oscar awards in the 1960s and 1970s. Simon specialized in witty urban situational comedies with a strong family component. Which brings us to the second of Goldie Hawn's successes in 1980, *Seems Like Old Times*, for which Simon wrote the screenplay. Here Hawn plays Glenda Parks, a Los Angeles defense attorney with a heart of gold. She defends habitual but harmless defendants like Native Americans Robert Brokenfeather and Thomas Jefferson Wolfcall, who she then hires to do odd jobs in the home she shares with her husband, district attorney Ira Parks (the ever-reliable Charles Grodin), who's hoping to clinch an appointment as attorney general. The complication in the story comes from her ex-husband Nick Gardenia (Chevy Chase, with whom Hawn starred in the 1978 hit *Foul Play*), an aspiring writer forced at gunpoint to commit a bank robbery by scheming criminals who then becomes a fugitive who hides out at the Parks family residence. Plenty of hijinks follow, among them Glenda's continuing attraction to Nick. Simon crafts an amusing ending, proficiently executed by Jay Sandrich, the veteran television director making his first and only foray into feature filmmaking. *Seems Like Old Times* is an old-fashioned, if sometimes zany, story about a love triangle. But at its center is a proficient professional woman who's a romantic at heart. As such the film represents a kind of cultural synthesis between feminist self-assertion and traditional romance, which was so typical of this transitional 1980 moment.

Amid these commercial Hollywood vehicles built to be crowd pleasers, there remained a cadre of fiercely independent filmmakers who continued to toil away pursuing personal visions of filmmaking, often garnering critical praise and sometimes attracting larger audiences while always at risk for marginality. There had always been such figures in Hollywood; D. W. Griffith, Orson Welles, Samuel Fuller, and, later, Spike Lee, come to mind as directors who could plausibly fall into this category. In an important respect, this maverick designation applies to the New Hollywood directors, with the crucial distinction that they were a self-consciously critical group who for a moment seemed to seize the spotlight in terms of influencing the direction of Hollywood from the late sixties through the late seventies. But even as they did so, there were older directors largely outside their ambit who had been quietly compiling a body of work with distinctive accents. Hal Ashby, who directed *Coming Home*, was one such figure. Woody Allen was another. In 1980, Allen was at the peak of his commercial power and cultural influence. And to at least some degree, he squandered it with *Stardust Memories*.

Allen, like Simon, cut his teeth on writing comedy (the two both worked as writers for early TV legend Sid Caesar). By the mid-sixties Allen was writing and directing his first movies, which reflected this sketch comedy sensibility. He turned a corner with *Annie Hall*, a romantic comedy starring himself and paramour Diane Keaton, which won Best Picture in 1977 and established him as a bona fide

cultural icon. (Not coincidentally, he was one of those fiercely independent artists who had a long-term contract with United Artists.)
Reflecting his newfound seriousness, Allen followed up *Annie Hall*
with the Ingmar Bermanesque *Interiors* in 1978, and his valentine to
his native New York, *Manhattan*, in 1979. Operating with peak autonomy in his final contractual commitment to UA (he would soon jump
ship to Orion, where his preferred executives had set up shop), Allen
embarked on the autobiographical *Stardust Memories*, a meditation
on stardom modeled on Federico Fellini's *8½* (Allen jokingly referred
to the film as "Woody Allen No. 4—I'm not even half of the Fellini
of *8½*.").[23]

Like *Manhattan*, *Stardust Memories* is shot in black-and-white, only
one indication of the way it pays homage to—but rejects the message
of—the 1941 Preston Sturges classic *Sullivan's Travels*. In that movie,
Joel McCrea plays a wildly successful Hollywood director who feels
he has a political obligation to make social dramas about the Great
Depression, and who, like Allen's character, is tired of making slapstick. Over the course of the story, he comes to understand that his
comic gift is his vocation and a genuine contribution he can make to
alleviate suffering in society. Allen's character, by contrast, insists on
rejecting mere humor, and preempts criticism by having characters
articulate the critique against him. "He's pretentious. His filming
style is too fancy. His insights are shallow and morbid. I've seen it all
before—they try to document their private suffering and pass it off as
art," says an executive played by *SNL* star Laraine Newman. Ironically, the best moments in the film are those that are purely comedic,
like the madcap Freudian scene from a movie-within-a-movie where
his character's escaped aggression goes on the loose, terrorizing the
people in his life, notably his mother. He also gets off a series of zippy
one-liners. "My mother was too busy running the chicken through
the de-flavorizing machine to think about shooting herself or anything," his character says of his culturally deprived childhood. "To
you, I'm an atheist," he tells one of the string of lovers in his life (here,
as in many Allen movies, infidelity and any number of other questionable behaviors are glossed over lightly). "To God, I'm the loyal

opposition." *Stardust Memories* marks the apotheosis of the Me Decade in Hollywood from its most successful practitioner.

To the extent that Allen gets political, there's a notably conservative thrust to the film. "I can never picture you, you know, hanging in there with the workers," he says in response to his lover's memories of her leftist youth, which have a distinctly limousine-liberal quality. "We were fighting for the spirit of things," she replies nostalgically, and not very convincingly, from the backseat of his chauffeured car.

In years to come, Allen directed some fine films, notably the wondrous *Purple Rose of Cairo* (1985), which truly does honor the spirit of Preston Sturges, and *Crimes and Misdemeanors* (1989), a profound meditation on the way crime goes unpunished. To the extent such movies succeeded, which could be considerably, they dropped the self-indulgent air that characterizes Allen's worst work.

When *Stardust Memories* was released on September 26, 1980, *Heaven's Gate* was almost ready. By then, its production had become a case study in throwing good money after bad, a project where Michael Cimino did just about everything to excess: he was excessively slow in shooting the movie, excessive in the sheer amount of footage that he shot, and excessive in the length of the picture he made (his final cut surged past his hard limit of three hours, itself commercially problematic, by forty minutes). He was also by many reckonings excessively imperious on the set, with his corporate overseers, and with the press (his nickname was "the Ayatollah"). By the time of the movie's premiere on November 18, the making of the movie had itself become a story—and a scandal—that colored its reception. A high-powered preview audience was conspicuously silent during the film's intermission, and there was a race for the exits when it was over. "Why aren't they drinking champagne?" Cimino asked a publicist at the reception following the screening. "Because they hate the movie, Michael," she replied. The executive who reported this conversation took pleasure in the gibe.[24]

She wasn't the only one. *Heaven's Gate*, opined *New York Times* reviewer Vincent Canby, "fails so completely that you might suspect Mr. Cimino sold his soul to the Devil to obtain the success of *The*

Deer Hunter, and the Devil has just come around to collect." Canby went on to pummel the film mercilessly before concluding that "*Heaven's Gate* is something quite rare in movies these days—an unqualified disaster.[25] "*GATE* GOES ON AND ON AND ON" read a headline in the New York *Post*. Andrew Sarris, known for the influential auteur theory that centered reception of a film around its director, called it "a ponderous spectacle." The reviews were equally bad outside New York and abroad, and they led some reviewers to reassess *The Deer Hunter* less positively than they previously had. One writer for *Rolling Stone* noted that "you get the feeling that these folks are not going to rest until they see Cimino behind bars."[26]

But the problem was far deeper than critical disapproval. After all, movies that critics hate become big hits all the time. It was that the failure of *Heaven's Gate* was indicative of a more fundamental problem, financial and otherwise, in a New Hollywood that seemed to have run its course. The movie's utter collapse itself became nationally notable, an item on the NBC Nightly News on November 20, when anchor John Chancellor cited "a bad day for United Artists." Crushed by the negative publicity, UA yanked *Heaven's Gate* from exhibition the next morning.[27] It also took the rare step of yanking it out of Cimino's hands, and hiring an outside editor to recut the film to under three hours. It was re-released in April 1981. But by then the damage had already been done. *Heaven's Gate* virtually wrecked Cimino's career—not entirely ending it, but never allowing him anything like the power and prestige he had enjoyed before its release (he died in relative obscurity in 2010). Largely silent at the time of its release, he later said, "I felt like *Heaven's Gate* was a beautiful, fantastically colored balloon tied to a string fastened to my wrist, so the balloon could never fly."[28] United Artists, by contrast, sank. In the wake of its $44 million failure,[29] Transamerica decided to wash its hands of its problematic investment, and sold the company to MGM, which absorbed UA's assets. The name survives; MGM resurrected UA as a subsidiary in 1987, and it currently exists as a digital studio. But it is now a mere bauble in the MGM stable and a shadow of its former self. Sometimes, works of art have observable, real-life consequences.

Was *Heaven's Gate* really that bad? The answer, in short, is no. A little harder to assess is how good it was.

The story is straightforward enough. Two old friends, James Averill (Kris Kristofferson) and Billy Irvine (John Hurt) cross paths twenty years after their 1870 graduation from Harvard in frontier Wyoming. But now they are on opposite sides in a brewing conflict between cattle barons and hard-bitten settlers who resort to rustling to survive. Kristofferson's Averill is a federal marshal sympathetic to the settlers, while Hurt's Irvine belongs to a cartel of the cattlemen. Irvine's friend Nate Champion (Walken) is an enforcer for the cattlemen and is tangled in a romantic triangle that pits him against Averill for the attentions of a bordello madam played by Huppert. A series of machinations ensue that culminate in a pitched battle in which there are a series of casualties among major characters. Averill survives, and we see him, clearly still haunted, in an epilogue set about a decade later in Newport, Rhode Island.

The first thing that needs to be said in any assessment of *Heaven's Gate* (we're talking here about Cimino's cut, the one that is now widely available) is that the film collected a remarkable array of talent, and much of that ability is evident onscreen. This includes the cinematography of Vilmos Zsigmond, the music of David Mansfield (composer of a lovely waltz for one of the set pieces of the film, in which he appears as fiddle player on roller skates), and, of particular note, the actors. The cast of *Heaven's Gate*—Kristofferson, Walken, Hurt, and Huppert, supplemented by Jeff Bridges, Sam Waterston, and a near-final appearance by the great Joseph Cotton—is uniformly excellent. Cimino himself also deserves praise for his panoramic shots of the western landscape and his fiercely observed interiors. The opening sequence in particular captures both the beauty and the stultifying quality of post–Civil War Harvard (even if it was shot at Oxford), and there is a magisterial quality to the film as a Western that as a whole gives the film a restorationist quality. Though its politics are conventionally liberal in terms of its David vs. Goliath plot, *Heaven's Gate* resembles the classic Westerns of John

Ford and George Stevens more than it does the films of Cimino's New Hollywood contemporaries.

All this said, the whole of *Heaven's Gate* doesn't quite add up to the sum of its parts. It really *is* long. And there's no major interpretative statement in the film resembling that of Fred Zinnemann's *High Noon* (an allegory of McCarthyism), Ford's *The Man Who Shot Liberty Valance* (with its avowedly troubling proposition of violence as the price of civilization), or, for that matter, Altman's *McCabe & Mrs. Miller* (which deconstructs the Western genre by focusing on its squalor). But if it isn't quite great, *Heaven's Gate* deserves to be taken seriously.

Which, belatedly, has happened. The film has been periodically released and discussed at film festivals and routinely shows up on various kinds of best lists. There is now a general perception that it was the victim of a piling-on effect in its initial reception. "I always suspected that maybe the movie got talked about too much beforehand," Christopher Walken said forty years later. "I was at that [November 18, 1980] screening, and I thought I'd watched a good movie."[30] The prestigious Criterion Collection added *Heaven's Gate* to its roster of films in 2012, and three years later critic Nicholas Barber, in an approving reappraisal, noted that the BBC listed it as #98 in the network's greatest American films of all time.[31]

As destructive as it was, *Heaven's Gate* did not single-handedly bring down New Hollywood. Many of the directorial stars who soared earlier in the seventies also produced colossal flops in the years that followed. For Steven Spielberg, it was *1941* (1979); for Francis Ford Coppola, it would be *One from the Heart* (1982); for George Lucas, it would be *Howard the Duck* (1986), though here he was producer rather than director. Martin Scorsese's *Raging Bull* was, and is, widely considered a masterpiece; four different film organizations dubbed it the best film of the 1980s, and many observers consider it the apex of Scorsese's professional achievements.[32] But it was nevertheless one of a string of box office disappointments that he directed, and as such was part of a larger reassessment undertaken by the powers that be in Hollywood. "The industry to a degree has abdicated to directors," Steven Bach told *The Wall Street Journal* at the time of *Heaven's Gate*'s release. "I think there is a general view that what a director does is quite a mysterious thing, and that when push comes to shove that mysterious vision must be allowed to operate without the kinds of strictures you would apply to a contractor who was building your swimming pool."[33] By 1980, such logic no longer applied. From that point on, the New Hollywood directors were on a much shorter leash—unless, like Spielberg and Lucas, they ran their own companies. Scorsese would go on to do distinguished work, but from here on out would depend on big stars, like Leonardo DiCaprio, to get them green-lighted.

There would be compensations, in New Hollywood and beyond. This is something that Coppola, a visionary in more ways than one, recognized as early as that Academy Awards ceremony in 1979. "I'd like to say that I think we're on the eve of something that's going to make the Industrial Revolution look like a small-town tryout out of town," Coppola stated in his remarks before he and Ali McGraw awarded Cimino his Oscar for Best Director. "I'm talking about the communications revolution. I think it's coming very quickly. And that the movies of the eighties are gonna be amazing beyond what any of you can dream just a couple years away from now. And I can see a communications revolution that is about movies, and art, and music, and digital electronics and computers and satellites, above all human talent. And it's gonna make things that the masters of the cinema from whom we've inherited this business wouldn't believe will be possible."[34] Though few viewers at the time could have fully understood what he was saying, it is clear that Coppola was anticipating a new world of special effects like computer-generated imagery, and perhaps the world of home video, the internet, and streaming that would soon transform Hollywood—and, perhaps, diminish its centrality in American popular culture, however pleasingly convenient so many of us regard such changes.

In any case, few critics or historians consider the eighties a golden age for Hollywood cinema the way the seventies were.[35] Another renaissance followed with the rise of small independent studios in the 1990s before they in turn were swallowed by larger studios.[36] Such is the ebb and flow of cinematic art. That is also why 1980 stands out. It is a good place to pause and note a changing cultural landscape whose features are so similar to, and so different than, our own.

DOMESTIC POLITICS

FIGURE 7. John Lennon and Yoko Ono, November 1980. After spending much of the seventies as a full-time husband and father—Ono managed his business empire—the couple returned to the pop scene at year's end with a new album, *Double Fantasy*. Its first hit single, with the tragically ironic title of "Starting Over," showed how, yet again, Lennon had tapped the zeitgeist, this time with a nod toward tradition that would become a major theme in eighties pop. (Jack Mitchell, Wikimedia Commons)

CHAPTER 4

Starting Over

Pop Music's Future Goes Back to the Past

JOHN LENNON WAS a househusband. His problem had a name: unrealized ambition.

Lennon, of course, had been one of the iconic media figures of the twentieth century. Emerging from obscurity in the early 1960s as the de facto leader of the British rock band The Beatles, he wrote or cowrote some of the most memorable pop music of his era, ranging from charming adolescent love songs like "I Wanna Hold Your Hand" (1964) to more meditative pieces like "In My Life" (1965), as well as experimental songs, such as "Strawberry Fields Forever" (1967), that pushed pop music to the very edges of the avant-garde. After the breakup of the Beatles at decade's end, he continued to blaze trails with fearlessly stark songs like "Mother" (1970) along with generational touchstones like "Imagine" (1972), a secular hymn that remains canonical in the twenty-first century. A vocal activist against the Vietnam War, Lennon spent years fighting a vindictive Nixon administration that tried to expel him from his adopted home of New York City. These difficulties were complicated by his tempestuous extramarital affair with the multimedia conceptual Japanese artist Yoko Ono, whom he married in 1969, but who evicted him from their Manhattan apartment in 1973, sending Lennon on an eighteen-month bender he called his "Lost Weekend." The two reunited in 1975, the same year their son Sean was born (each had a child from a previous

75

marriage). Lennon spent the next five years based on the Upper West Side of Manhattan in the landmark Dakota building on 72nd Street, baking bread—"it was like an album coming out of the oven," he boasted—running neighborhood errands, and taking his toddler for swimming lessons.[1]

In this, too, he was a singular figure. His former bandmates Paul McCartney, George Harrison, and Ringo Starr continued their musical careers, McCartney in particular enjoying sustained success with his new band, Wings, co-fronted with his wife Linda, a well-known photographer. Friendly rivals like Bob Dylan and Mick Jagger remained as visible in the 1970s as they had in the sixties. But Lennon stood out by dropping out. "I wasn't really enjoying what I was doing," he explained in a November 1980 profile in the *New York Times*. "I was a machine that was supposed to produce so much creative *something* and give it out periodically for approval to justify my existence on earth." Lennon asserted that becoming a stay-at-home-dad gave his life a new sense of purpose. "When I look at the relative importance of what life is about, I can't quite convince myself that making a record or having a career is more important than my child, or any child."[2]

If this was the truth, it wasn't the whole truth. For one thing, as Lennon recognized, his domestic life was a notably cosseted one. "I'm a housewife who also has a nanny and an assistant and a cook and a cleaner," he acknowledged. (And that was just for starters.) For another, his musical retirement was not exactly voluntary in that he found himself with a paucity of material—and inspiration. Lennon had been quite productive in the first half of the seventies, releasing six albums. Two of them, *John Lennon/Plastic Ono Band* (1970) and *Imagine* (1972), contain songs that are widely considered to hold up as well as anything he recorded with The Beatles. Lennon also collaborated with two of the most celebrated figures of the decade, David Bowie (with whom he cowrote Bowie's chart-topping 1973 hit "Fame" with guitarist Carlos Alomar) and Elton John (their duet, "Whatever Gets You Through the Night" also went to number one the following year).[3] But Lennon's creative juices largely dried up after that. In 1975, he released *Rock & Roll*, an anthology of cover tunes from the rock stars of his youth—a classic move by performers running on fumes or fulfilling a contract (Lennon was both). He seemed to be out of things to say, musically and otherwise.

He wasn't quite happy about it. A former art school student, Lennon was an adept sketch artist whose two books, *In His Own Write* (1964) and *A Spaniard in the Words* (1965) were filled with literary and visual drawings. His self-portrait for his thirty-eighth birthday in 1978 bore a revealing caption: "The hole of my life flashed before my eyes." Throughout that year and 1979, Lennon noodled in various forms without coming up with anything complete, his musical fragments including a satirical dig at Bob Dylan ("I'm stuck inside of a lexicon with the *Roget's Thesaurus* blues again") reminiscent of his 1970 attack on Paul McCartney, "How Do You Sleep" (with its jibe "the only thing you done was yesterday"), indicative of his insecurities. Beatles scholar Kenneth Womack may have been exaggerating, but not by much, when he asserted that Lennon's "hiatus from the music business hadn't come about because he wanted to stay home and raise his infant son—a story he had repeated to almost everyone he knew—but rather, because he had lost his muse." Womack asserts that "what John really wanted was to regain his spark."[4]

John and Yoko—their celebrity as a couple led them to be widely referenced on a first-name basis—spent much of the late seventies traveling as tourists and visiting their homes on Long Island and in Palm Beach. A trip to Bermuda in the summer of 1980 proved pivotal, as the various fragments Lennon had been producing began to cohere. Yoko, who managed John's musical career, made discreet queries about recording, mindful of his fragile ego and determined to give him an out if things didn't go well. She approached a producer that the couple had worked with previously, Jack Douglas, who had since enjoyed success with the rock bands Aerosmith and Cheap Trick. In August 1980, the couple began working at The Hit Factory, a studio on the west side of Manhattan.[5]

The record that resulted, *Double Fantasy*—the title refers to a variety of freesia abundant in Bermuda, as well as their own inner states—was an autobiographical portrait of a marriage in which each member gets equal space. As such, the album is a feminist manifesto. John's track "Cleanup Time," for example, describes Yoko in the counting house while he labors in the kitchen, a pointed inversion of traditional gender roles.

Lennon's avowed egalitarianism is all the more striking given his own self-professed history of violent misogyny. One can glimpse it, for example, in his chilling 1965 song from *Rubber Soul*, "Run for Your Life," in which he warns a lover that if he catches her with another man, "that's the end, little girl." In "Getting Better," from the 1967 album *Sgt. Pepper's Lonely Hearts Club Band*, Lennon sings, "I used to be cruel to my woman and beat her and kept her apart from the things that she loved," a line he cited as autobiographical. "I was a hitter," he told *Playboy*.[6]

By 1980, however, Lennon had long since come to a place where professing vulnerability came naturally to him, and this is evident on *Double Fantasy*. "My life is in your hands," he says to Yoko in "Woman." The famous image of a naked Lennon cleaving to a fully dressed Yoko in the *Rolling Stone* cover of 1980 is indicative of his gender position, one that suggests the degree to which he had fully absorbed the tenets of seventies-style liberal feminism—reflected, in ways that include its excesses, in his 1972 song "Woman Is the N——of the World," for which he received an approving citation from the National Organization of Women.[7]

Such seventies currents notwithstanding, *Double Fantasy* nevertheless anticipated cultural shifts that would become more pronounced in the coming decade. This is clear in the most fundamental statement the record makes: it is an affirmation of what would soon be called "family values," in which heterosexual monogamy gets pride of place and child-rearing is at the very heart of the meaning of life. Lennon the social activist is entirely missing here: "There's no problems, only solutions," he tells those who feel he should again be promoting utopian visions in "Watching the Wheels." In fact, there had always been a vein of skepticism toward reform, personal as well as political, in Lennon's thought, seen in his hesitation to follow George Harrison in embracing the Maharishi Mahesh Yogi's Transcendental Meditation when the Beatles went to India in 1968 or in his response to those who sought institutional change in his classic anti-anthem "Revolution" (1968): "You better change your mind instead." Lennon was nevertheless at the radical edge of the counterculture at the turn of the seventies—associated with figures like Abbie Hoffman, Jerry Rubin, and Bobby Seale—a position he explicitly renounced a decade later. "That radicalism was phony, really, out of guilt," he told *Newsweek* as part of the run-up to the album's release. "I'd always felt guilty that I'd made money, so I had to give it away or lose it." Lennon described himself as a "chameleon" who "became whoever I was with."[8]

It was perhaps a measure of Lennon's cultural antennae that the most important dimension of his emerging conservatism was musical. Viewed from one angle, this is perhaps not surprising. In the mid-sixties, Lennon had been at the vanguard of musical innovation, influenced by cutting-edge composers like Karlheinz Stockhausen and borrowing from Ono's work with John Cage in the musique concrete-styled "Revolution #9" (1968). But the general trend in his work was toward a leaner, more stripped-down sound in his late Beatles songs and his music of the early seventies. What's a little surprising about *Double Fantasy* is just how hook-laden, how *pop*-minded, so many of the songs are. This was very much a conscious decision. "Another thing those five years did for me was to move a lot of intellectual garbage out of the way," he told *Times* house music critic Robert Palmer. "For me, a lot of the so-called avant-garde in pop is pseudo-intellectual—which is something I contributed to. Basically, you just want a good record, right?"[9] Interestingly, this ethos was reflected in Ono's contributions to the album as well. While her keening vocal style (one that includes simulating sexual climax in "Kiss Kiss") was never exactly accessible, her songs on the album are more melodic than her earlier recordings; Lennon plausibly cited the work of singers like Kate Pierson of the B-52s—another band that found success with a spare, simple style in the eighties—as inheritors of her musical approach.

The apotheosis of the new, which is to say old, Lennon, was the lead single from *Double Fantasy*, "(Just Like) Starting Over." An exquisitely produced piece of pop craft—it sonically shimmers with a crispness that sounds fresh, even now—the song is nevertheless a very self-conscious throwback, rendered in a form that harkens back to Roy Orbison and (especially) Elvis Presley, right down to phrases like "well, well, darlin.'" This sense of paradox is reflected in the lyrics of the song as well, which express an almost adolescent sense of yearning coupled with the encroachments of middle age ("It's been so long since we took the time / No one's to blame, time flies so quickly"). If the song is marked by nostalgia, it is also marked by urgency and loss: it'll be *just like* starting over. Not quite the same thing. But close.

"I'd done that music and identified with it," Lennon told *Playboy*, referring both to his early days covering the work of rock and roll pioneers of the fifties while playing on the club circuit in the sixties and his recordings of their songs on the *Rock & Roll* album in the seventies. "But I've never written a song that sounded like that period. So I just thought, why the hell not? In the Beatles days that would have been taken as a joke. One avoided clichés. 'Course now clichés are not clichés anymore."[10]

Clichés are not clichés anymore: Lennon encapsulated what so much of the coming decade would be about. He couldn't have fully known this of course, and as this tiny snapshot of his career makes clear, he was very much a man in, and of, the seventies. But in the uncanny way that the best pop artists do, Lennon seemed to feel his way toward where the culture was headed.

And then he was murdered.

Although it's not well remembered now, the pop music business in 1980 was not in good shape. The downturn had begun in 1979, when sales fell 11 percent. This figure was all the more notable given the steady growth of the industry in good times and bad, and because the preceding years had been marked by blockbuster releases, such as Fleetwood Mac's *Rumors* (1977), as well as the *Saturday Night Fever* (1977) and *Grease* (1978) soundtracks, all of which rank among the bestselling albums of all time. Different reasons were offered for the decline, among them the sharp recession caused by the energy crisis of 1979, the rise of home recording on audio cassettes, and competition from new media, such as video games. There was some belief that the industry had reached a saturation point.[11]

From the standpoint of the twenty-first century, it was a different, and simpler, world. Its twin pillars were retail sales and radio airplay, which were mutually reinforcing. The dominant format was the so-called LP, or long-playing, or 33-rpm (rotations per minute) vinyl record, which could hold about forty-five minutes of music (about twenty minutes on each grooved side). In pop music, the LP had long since been referred to as an "album," borrowing a metaphor from photography, in which a collection of discrete musical snapshots added up to more than the sum of its parts. Frank Sinatra had pioneered this idea as early as the 1940s, which crystallized in his classic 1954 album *In the Wee Small Hours*, taking the idea to its logical conclusion in forging a thematically unified "concept" album of related songs (in this case, music for late at night). But it was The Beatles who broke the concept album wide open with *Sgt. Pepper*, which became the benchmark for all that followed. By the end of the sixties, the album had displaced the 45-rpm "single" (a featured song on its A-side; a more minor one on the B-side) as the most profitable and influential way pop music was experienced, though singles remained important drivers of album sales and radio formats. There were other formats as well, notably the 8-track tape, which was popular for listening to music in cars, and the prerecorded audiocassette, which was growing in popularity and which by 1984 would overtake the LP as the most profitable of all formats.

In an important sense, 1980 was the end of an era. In 1981, Music Television, or MTV, would make its debut as a channel on cable television and would transform the industry in multiple ways, among them a new emphasis on visual—more crudely, sex—appeal, and a new emphasis on hit songs as the primary driver of sales in the music business. In the years that followed, compact disks, file sharing, streaming, and any number of other ways of hearing and distributing songs emerged. The net effect of such innovations have made pop

music much more widely available; they have also made it significantly less profitable, since it has become something one rarely buys
directly anymore. It used to be that tours were mounted to promote
records; now it is the other way around. Once upon a time, record col-
lections were hard-won acts of personal curation, built over time and
at considerable expense; now anything you'd ever care to hear is a
click away. The same might be said of the hardware apparatus for listening to music. In 1980, stereo systems were often large, loud, and a
point of personal pride for those who built and maintained them.
Now a listener might have any number of devices, more likely than
not primarily used for other purposes, which can also play music.

The year 1980 was a turning point in pop music in other ways as
well. Two of the musical subgenres that had dominated the seventies,
disco and punk rock, were on the wane in terms of sales, influence,
and reputation. Yet both retained some degree of potency, and both
also seemed to adjust to a shifting cultural wavelength as one decade
gave way to another.[12]

Disco was the sound of the city: a racially diverse, technology-
driven, slickly produced musical form that exploited repetition and
nightclub associations to achieve a hypnotic effect. Musically, it was a
direct descendant of rhythm and blues; culturally, it had strong ties
to gay communities. What made it distinctive was its emphasis on
danceability, which came from a combination of the beat (especially
in its use of the high hat), wah-wah guitar licks, and conga percussion,
among other elements. By the mid-seventies disco had become a
global fad, evident in novelty hits like Memphis disk-jockey Rick
Dees's "Disco Duck" (1976) to the Dominic Monardo (aka. Meco)
disco version of the Star Wars theme, which became a hit in 1977.

There were a number of disco acts, like the multiracial KC and the
Sunshine Band, that achieved stardom with a series of hits within
the genre. But disco achieved mainstream mass appeal in the late
1970s with the release of the 1977 movie Saturday Night Fever and
its soundtrack album featuring the Australian trio the Bee Gees, a
1960s rock group who reinvented themselves for the disco era. Yet even
as disco was peaking in popular appeal, racism and homophobia—

typified by the young white male slogan "Disco Sucks!"—sought to counteract it. But disco had a deep and enduring influence on popular music, even on rock, which was the source of much of the hostility against it. A disco dimension was unmistakable in the Rolling Stones' 1978 single "Miss You" (released, as many songs of the era were, in an extended disco version), for example, and became a musical pillar in the career of crossover artists like Madonna, though by this point the term had fallen out of common usage in favor of the more generic, and perhaps less polarizing, "dance music." Beyond the racial and sexual countercurrents that buffeted it, disco was largely played out as a musical fad, even among its most ardent champions, by decade's end, notwithstanding the release of durably beloved classics like Sister Sledge's "We Are Family" (1979), written and musically backed by Nile Rodgers and Bernard Edwards, the hitmakers who fronted their own band, Chic.[13]

No figure better embodied the ethos of disco—and successfully repositioned herself in its wake—than Donna Summer. Widely known as "the Queen of Disco," Summer burst into international fame in 1975 on the strength of her hit "Love to Love You Baby," notable for Italian producer Giorgio Moroder's use of synthesizers and Summer's orgasmic moaning. She went on to enjoy an unbroken string of hits in the next four years, which included the pulsating "I Feel Love" (1977), a remake of pop craftsman Jimmy Webb's "MacArthur Park" (1978), and "Dim All the Lights" (1979), which she wrote herself. No pop star was bigger than she was in these years.

But Summer was restless by 1980. Her desire to break out of what she increasingly considered a disco straitjacket was evident in her 1979 hit "Hot Stuff," a bona fide rock song with a searing guitar solo by former Doobie Brother and Steely Dan member Jeff "Skunk" Baxter. The song came from Bad Girls, a double album indicative of Summer's growing musical ambition. But her desire to reset was more than simply musical; a committed Christian always uneasy with her image as a sex symbol, Summer underwent a born-again experience in 1979 that reconnected her with her gospel roots.[14] She was also unhappy with her working relationship with the disco-heavy label

Casablanca Records and was eager to work with music impresario David Geffen, who was starting a record label in his own name. (Geffen also landed Lennon as a client; *Double Fantasy* was among the first releases on his fledgling label.)

The result was Summer's 1980 album *The Wanderer*, a snapshot of a career in transition. The title track, a straight R & B number alluding to Dion's 1961 classic of the same name, was the first single off the album and hit number three on the *Billboard* chart. Other tracks, like "Cold Love" and "Who Do You Think You're Foolin'" had a heavy-metal crunch that were indicative of a new direction, though not one with as much popular appeal, as the two only managed to reach the bottom of the Top 40. More revealing still was the closing track on the album, "I Believe in Jesus," a gospel tune with rock accents—a statement of sorts, and a bold one at that given the challenge it implicitly posed to her core audience. Summer would ultimately revitalize her career in the early eighties with hits like "Love Is in Control" (1982), and, especially, "She Works Hard for the Money" (1983), a song that shows how thoroughly she had exchanged her ethereal sex goddess identity for a more down-to-earth persona.

Disco may have been dying in 1980, but the year did see the release of some real classic songs in its canon. Significantly, though, they did not come from the usual places. One of the biggest songs of the year was "Funkytown," by the interracial Minneapolis band Lipps Inc. "Funkytown" had an unmistakable disco rhythm, though its ten-note hook owed more to an emerging strain of synth pop that would come to dominate the eighties.

Minneapolis, whose vibrant musical scene made it a cultural capital of sorts at the turn of the decade, was also the home base for one of the most protean figures in the history of popular music: Prince. Like all great artists, Prince resisted musical pigeonholing; he was, among other things, a songwriter of first rank (for himself and others), a legendary guitarist, a versatile singer, and a mesmerizing live performer. A musical prodigy who studied the record industry from a young age—he signed his first contract when he was nineteen years old—Prince was also notable for his wide range of musical influences, disco

DYNAMIC DUO

FIGURE 8. Michael Jackson and Quincy Jones at the time of *Off the Wall*, released in 1979 and spawning hits into 1980. The album marked a crucial career passage between Jackson's years as a child prodigy with the Jackson Five and the astounding global celebrity he achieved with *Thriller* in 1982. Jones was a legend in his own right as a producer for a series of artists that ranged from Frank Sinatra to Aretha Franklin. (Photofest)

among them.[15] His first album, *For You*, was released in 1978; he followed it with *Prince* in 1979, whose sexually charged debut single "I Wanna Be Your Lover," hit number eleven in December of that year. He followed it in 1980 with *Dirty Mind*, whose lead single "Uptown" also bore clear disco influences even as it has a rock and funk tilt that was hard to pin down. By this point, Prince was widely hailed in critical circles as a performer on the cusp of greatness, hopes that would soon be realized in his classic albums *1999* (1982) and *Purple Rain* (1984). This work cemented his place alongside Michael Jackson, Bruce Springsteen, and Madonna (whose work also owed a lot to disco) as one of the titans of eighties pop.

Jackson was at the tail end of a metamorphosis himself in 1980, and one in which disco played an important role. Another musical prodigy, he had been best known as the irresistibly charming front boy of the Jackson 5, part of a final flowering of Motown Records in the early seventies that also included the Commodores and their lead singer Lionel Ritchie. In an ambitious self-conscious step toward emancipating himself both from his family and from his label, Jackson teamed up with the esteemed producer Quincy Jones and released *Off the Wall* in the summer of 1979. Its first single, "Don't Stop 'Til You Get Enough," was the apotheosis of disco in its danceability and message of self-gratification. In January 1980, another disco-inflected single, "Rock with You," went to number one, inaugurating what would be one of the greatest decades of commercial success in the history of popular music. Jackson spent the first half of 1980 at the top of the pop charts with two more hits, the similarly danceable title track as well as the mournful ballad "She's Out of My Life." He was thus already a superstar when the release of *Thriller* in 1982 shot him into the pop culture pantheon.

There was another Motown alumna in 1980 whose career also blossomed, and also because of a fortuitous partnership: Diana Ross, erstwhile lead singer of the Supremes, the marquee act of the label in its sixties heyday, with disco hitmakers Chic. After early success on her own, Ross had been fading over the course of the seventies, but she roared back in 1980 with her album *Diana*, in which Chic was her backing band. Nile Rodgers and Bernard Edwards crafted the almost impossibly catchy hits "Upside Down" and "I'm Coming Out" (whose main riff was resurrected seventeen years later in the Notorious B.I.G.'s posthumous number one song "Mo Money Mo Problems"). Ross would top the charts once more in 1981 with "Endless Love" from the movie of the same name, but *Diana* was the high-water mark of her solo career, and it extended her reign as pop music royalty for the remainder of the century.

The other important fading pop music subgenre in 1980 was punk rock. Punk was an Anglo-American phenomenon. In Britain, the dominant emotion was rage, expressed most forcefully and thrillingly by the Sex Pistols, whose sole album, *Nevermind the Bollocks Here's the Sex Pistols* (1977) reinvented rock and roll by contemptuously rejecting the idea of convention, artistry, and the encrusted weight of pretense that had come to characterize much of the rock world by the mid-1970s by so-called progressive rock bands like Pink Floyd, Yes, Jethro Tull, and their baroque, elaborately produced, imitators. The Sex Pistols could barely play their instruments, but songs like "Anarchy in the UK" and "God Save the Queen" (banned by the British Broadcasting Corporation) embodied the anger of young Britain in the throes of economic decline.[16]

The Sex Pistols' torch was carried forward by the Clash, a more ambitious and focused punk rock band. The Clash was part of the original punk scene in London in the mid-seventies, releasing their eponymous debut album in 1977, one that included a cover version of the classic 1966 Bobby Fuller Four song "I Fought the Law." Their second album, *Give 'Em Enough Rope*—a reference to the famous maxim attributed to Vladimir Lenin that "the capitalists will sell us rope with which to hang them"—followed a year later, and was highly topical, addressing domestic and international politics from an avowedly Marxist standpoint. But it was with *London Calling*, released in Britain in late 1979 and in the United States in 1980, that the band made its commercial breakthrough, selling five million copies and leading to the band's first hit single, "Train in Vain," whose title alludes to a canonical blues tune by Mississippi Delta guitarist Robert Johnson.

London Calling was notable for its wide range of global musical influences, a tendency that continued to characterize the band even as it remained anchored in a rock idiom.

The most important inheritor of the punk mantle was the Irish band U2. The band's first album, *Boy*, came out in October 1980. A militantly pacifist quartet consisting of Catholic and Protestant members growing up in the times of the "the Troubles," U2 performed with figurative—and, in some cases, actual—religious zeal, a spirit reflected in "I Will Follow," a single from the album. While the band initially forged an evocative, signature sound built on repetition, its sonic vocabulary rapidly evolved, making U2 the most popular rock band in the world by the end of the eighties, extending punk's legacy but bending it in accessible and traditional directions (band members were passionate devotees of what was rapidly becoming American roots music, from Elvis Presley to Billie Holiday).

In contrast with what came out of the UK, American punk rock often had a more playful spirit, along with the hard-edged sound apparent in West Coast bands, such as X, fronted by the charismatic Exene Cervenka. But the U.S. movement was centered in downtown New York, where bands such as the Ramones made loud, fast, short songs whose simplicity was irresistible. (They *sounded* like the Sex Pistols, but were usually a good deal sillier, as their 1978 signature song "I Wanna Be Sedated" suggests.) But by 1980, punk rock was giving way to a newer variant, known as new wave, which had begun to emerge in the late seventies.

New wave bore a clear resemblance to punk with its avowedly brash style and an impatience with the pretensions of traditional rock music. But it placed more emphasis on catchy riffs and commercial success than the rebels whose professed ambivalence about the record industry could be pretentious (if not hypocritical) in its own right. Early British examples of new wave included the Buzzcocks and the remarkably prolific—and angrily clever—Elvis Costello, who became a critical darling upon the release of his debut album *My Aim Is True* in 1977. In 1980, Costello released his fourth LP, *Get Happy!*, whose retro packaging and embrace of soul music suggested the incipient allure of tradition for a performer whose use of the word "happy" was rarely other than an expression of irony.

It was an Ohioan on the British scene—Chrissie Hynde, founder of the Pretenders—who forged a powerful Anglo-American fusion that combined an unmistakable punk stance, hook-laden songs, and an unapologetically feminist perspective. The Pretenders, born from odds and ends on the London scene, released their self-titled debut album in January 1980. Hard-edged and profane, the album nevertheless finished in the Top 20 albums of the year, and generated a hit single, "Brass in Pocket," that would make Hynde one of the signature voices of the eighties. Like other new wave bands, the Pretenders would evolve in more of a pop direction without ever entirely losing its punk edge.

In 1980 new wave really solidified and became a powerful commercial force in pop music. And it was two acts from the downtown New York punk scene who rode it most successfully and durably. In terms of critical acclaim and lasting influence, the premier new wave band was Talking Heads. A foursome led by the Rhode Island School of Design graduate David Byrne, this cerebral band's first album, *Talking Heads '77*, spawned its cult classic song "Psycho Killer," sung from the point of view of a mentally ill man. They followed that album with *More Songs about Buildings and Food* in 1978, from which they had their first hit single, a strangely slow, even aberrant, cover version of soul singer Al Green's song "Take Me to the River." And in 1979's *Fear of Music*, they released what some consider their signature song, "Life During Wartime," in which a nervous undercover operative involved in potentially dangerous activities utters a line that became a meme: "This ain't no party, this ain't no disco, this ain't no foolin' around."

In 1980 Talking Heads released the landmark album on which the band's critical reputation rests, *Remain in Light*. A collaboration with cutting edge producer Brian Eno, who introduced bandmembers to Nigerian bandleader Fela Kuti, the album is a startlingly original fusion of Afrobeat (a musical idiom combining African and Caribbean sources), synthesizer-based rock, and allusive lyrics that took popular music to the very edges of intelligibility even as it remained arrestingly memorable. ("Lost my shape / trying to act casual," goes the opening line from one song, "Crosseyed and Painless.") The highlight of the record is the generational anthem "Once in a Lifetime," rendered from the point of view of a materialistic suburbanite musing on his existence amid aqueous rhythms and a guitar line that seems to pull him down. *Remain in Light* is very much an album of the seventies in its critical stance toward American mythology. And yet, within a few years, in their albums *Speaking in Tongues* (1983), *Little Creatures* (1985), and *True Stories* (1986), the Talking Heads would plunge headlong into an affectionate love affair with Americana, typified by songs like "Road to Nowhere," "Creatures of Love," and Wild Life," whose lyrics were sometimes ambiguous but whose zesty arrangements included dashes of white gospel and country in its musical gumbo.

But the most successful new wave band—probably the most successful pop band of all in 1980—was Blondie. This talented group of musicians, fronted by the stylishly brazen Deborah Harry, made a name for itself in the downtown New York scene, where the group's members rubbed shoulders with the Talking Heads and the Ramones, among other punk acts. But in making the transition to new wave, none of Blondie's peers had a more unerring edge for crafting catchy pop tunes. The first in the band's string of number one songs was "Heart of Glass," yet another example of disco's lingering allure. Other hits followed, among them the bestselling single of the year, "Call Me," the theme song from the movie *American Gigolo*, starring sex symbol Richard Gere. Notably, the song was produced by Giorgio Moroder, of Donna Summer fame. Sung from the point of view of a concupiscent woman seeking a tryst, "Call Me" was marked by a slashing, muscular guitar line, culminating in a chorus in which Harry lustily shouts the title of the song. Her charismatic persona stemmed from the way she managed to combine a delicate voice with a sense of heedless abandon. These qualities were apparent in the band's album *Eat to the Beat*, which was released in 1979 but finished as the eighth best-selling album of 1980, led by the hit single "Dreaming," whose strong reverb made Harry's voice both powerful and ethereal.

Blondie attained the zenith of its pop power with *Autoamerican*, an album released in November 1980. The record contained a pair of chart-topping hits that were indicative of the band's unerring feel for the pulse of pop culture on the fulcrum of the new decade. The first, "The Tide Is High," was a remake of the 1967 calypso song by the Paragons, a Jamaican band, to which Harry added another one of her trademark confident vocals as she switched the song's perspective from male to female—an important interpretive statement captured in her purring voice. The band's decision to cover a calypso tune was indicative of a larger fascination with Caribbean music among many white pop artists, ranging from Eric Clapton to the Clash, who had hits with songs with clear reggae influences. (Calypso, a West Indian musical form, has a more secular cast than reggae, which originated in Jamaica and has strong ties to the religious culture of Rastafarianism.) By 1980, reggae had become an internationally famous style, thanks in no small part to the music of Bob Marley, a Jamaican singer-songwriter and bandleader who rose to international fame in the 1970s before his tragically premature death from cancer in 1981. Out of this tangled, overlapping set of musical idioms came the 1980s genre of world beat, of which one could plausibly say that Blondie was a pioneer.

Blondie's other big hit from *Autoamerican*, "Rapture," was a takeoff on the emerging idiom of hip-hop, in which Harry performed a credible rap (albeit one that would later be dismissed by some as mere cultural appropriation). A video version of the song featured rapper Fab Five Freddy—who is mentioned in the song—and graffiti artists Lee Quiñones and Jean-Michel Basquiat, himself still a few years from art-world stardom. Unfortunately, Blondie's fortunes came crashing down in the early eighties amid internal conflicts and member Chris Stein's affliction with a rare skin disorder, leading paramour Harry to also stop performing. The band later regrouped but never recovered its commercial momentum.

The success of "Rapture" reflected the gathering strength of an infant musical genre that soon took the world by storm. It is important to note that early hip-hop—or rap, to use a once more common term—was not only, or even primarily, about making records. Actually, it connoted a larger set of cultural practices that began to emerge in the mid-1970s. One was the use of graffiti, a practice of painting public spaces in a personal style that often involved a literal or figurative signature. Another was the creation of a form of dance known as b-boy, or break dancing, which involved stylish poses and the use of hands to support one's body at least as much as feet. A distinctive style of music known as dub—a reggae variant that involved remixing of records by playing two simultaneously—often accompanied break dancing. Dub rapidly evolved via mixing rhythm tracks, scratching needles on records, and sampling pop-music songs with a pair of turntables, as well as improvisational speech—known as toasting—by an emcee, or MC, who worked alongside the disc jockey, or DJ (sometimes the same person). Though its musical origins were largely Caribbean, a key site of this vital subculture was anchored in the New York City borough of the Bronx, where black, Latino, and other racial and ethnic influences converged. One pioneer of this emerging style was the Jamaican-born rapper Kool Herc, who became famous for his work as a DJ at block parties and clubs. Other key figures in this protean moment included Afrika Bambaataa and Melle Mel, all of whom were still largely invisible to the general public in 1980 while laying the groundwork for a musical revolution.[17]

One irony here is that the recording many historians consider the first hit hip-hop record, the Sugar Hill Gang's "Rapper's Delight" (1979), which reached the bottom of the *Billboard* Top 40 in January 1980, came not out of the Bronx but New Jersey. When entrepreneur Sylvia Robinson, who owned a recording studio, failed to convince prominent Bronx rappers to make a record, her son recruited a trio of unknowns to record a song that drew heavily on Chic's 1979 hit "Good Times" (resulting in the first of many lawsuits that grew out of the hip-hop ethos of sampling). "Rapper's Delight" demonstrated the tremendous potential of rap. By the end of the eighties, it displaced rock and roll as the culturally dominant genre in popular music.

Like most forms of popular culture, pop music derives from a struggle to square a circle of novelty and tradition: you want a song to be both fresh and familiar at the same time. In a typical pop hit, the accent is on the former: novelty is what propels a song into prestige, sales, and influence, even while the familiar offers a listener a sense of bearings as well as comfort. In country music, however, the accent is more on tradition, which must be honored and affirmed—even rebelliousness tends to have a pedigree—in the struggle to find something new to say. Fears of selling out, dilution, or cheap appropriation often hover over discussions of all pop music genres, but a concern about fakery is especially widespread in country, even when—especially when—crossover acts enjoy commercial success.

Few country aficionados would cite the year 1980 as a high-water mark of the genre. To be sure, there were long-standing acts with sterling credentials of authenticity who remained active, among them Johnny Cash, Dolly Parton, Loretta Lynn, and the so-called Outlaws—frequent collaborators Merle Haggard, Waylon Jennings, and Willie Nelson. Jennings's theme song from the hit TV series *The Dukes of Hazzard* placed in the top ten country songs of the year, as did Nelson's "On the Road Again" and "My Heroes Have Always Been Cowboys." George Jones, whose famously tempestuous marriage to Tammy Wynette resulted in a string of hit duets, enjoyed a smash solo hit in 1980 with the beloved classic "He Stopped Loving Her Today"—the day in question being the day the song's protagonist died.

Nevertheless, the dominant discourse in country music was an ongoing debate about whether the form's accommodation of pop music trappings—in the use of orchestral strings as a backdrop, or rock flourishes in the foreground, for example—compromised its integrity. The most notorious expression of this conflict came at the Country Music Awards of 1975, when old-guard presenter Charlie Rich set the card giving folksy hitmaker John Denver the "Entertainer of the Year" award on fire.[18] The tension was rarely that dramatic or literal; indeed, artists like Parton, who enjoyed a smash pop chart topper with the theme song from *9 to 5* in 1980, had few compunctions about wandering into commercial territory (vividly demonstrating how you could take the girl out of the holler, but you could never take the holler out of the girl). Parton's other hit of 1980,

"Starting Over Again," went to number one on the country charts—and, ironically, was cowritten by Donna Summer and her husband, Bruce Sudano. Parton would provide a form of musical payback when her 1973 ballad "I Will Always Love You" became one of the biggest pop hits of all time for Whitney Houston in 1992. Such cross-cultural exchanges demonstrate the futility of insisting on artistic purity in popular music.

The biggest country music phenomenon of 1980 was the release of the *Urban Cowboy* soundtrack. While the movie was a hit, the album was a blockbuster, and in its wake, there was talk of an "Urban Cowboy" movement marked by bolo ties and the popularity of Gilley's, a Texas nightclub where the film was shot and which became a tourist attraction after the film's release (it burned down in 1990).[19] Owner Mickey Gilley, cousin of fifties rocker Jerry Lee Lewis, was also a country music star. While the new vogue for this scene suggested the ways that country music was getting slicker, it is also a reflection of movement in the other direction—a new cohort of music fans seeking to move away from the glitz and glitter of other pop genres toward something that seemed more natural and authentic.

Reflecting these crosscurrents, the *Urban Cowboy* soundtrack offered a snapshot of how sprawling a domain country music had become by 1980. It spawned three chart-topping pop singles: Johnny Lee's "Lookin' for Love," Gilley's "Stand by Me," and Anne Murray's "Could I Have this Dance" (Murray, a Canadian, was the kind of pop singer that made country purists chafe). Other hits included "Love the World Away," by Kenny Rogers, who straddled country and pop and who had the number one country song of the year in "Coward of the County." Charlie Daniels, situated between country and rock, appeared with his band in the movie, and had a big hit in 1979 with "The Devil Went Down to Georgia." He then followed it up in 1980 with his truculently patriotic anthem "In America." The song was a clear indication of the way many southern working-class whites, who had for generations considered themselves Democrats, were beginning to embrace an avowed conservatism in their politics, musical and otherwise.

But *Urban Cowboy* also featured performers for whom a country label would be a stretch at best. Boz Scaggs, a bluesy rock performer, scored a hit with "Look at What You've Done to Me." Joe Walsh, a flamboyant rock guitarist, also landed in the Top 40 with "All Night Long." Walsh by that point had become a member of the Eagles, a country-rock band that had since made the transition to rock, as had vocalist Linda Ronstadt. They too appeared on the *Urban Cowboy* soundtrack. Yet another erstwhile country artist, Aussie Olivia Newton-John, had no country trace of her left in 1980, when she spent four weeks at number one with "Magic," the theme song from the movie *Xanadu.* While Nashville was for some a lifelong destination, others found a home there later in their careers (Elvis Presley is a good example) and still others would make it a point of departure (a more contemporary example would be Taylor Swift).

Amid the waxing and waning of pop music genres and subgenres in 1980, however, a center still held. Pop music historians often lament that in contrast to the sixties, the music of the 1970s was marked by increasing segregation of audiences, especially on radio, where so much of hit-making was decided. This is true. But there remained a battery of longtime performers who commanded broad audiences in a shared culture that was less fragmented than it would be in decades to come. They were also often able to blend musical styles in distinctive ways. Years before his touchstone album *Graceland* fused African and American musical styles with startling freshness, sixties stalwart Paul Simon released his film and album *One-Trick Pony* in 1980, which featured his marvelous, rhythmically supple top ten hit "Late in the Evening."

Two other acts who commanded broad genre and generational appeal were the Eagles and Linda Ronstadt—the former at one point had been the backing band for the latter. The Eagles, who had pioneered a brand of introspective country-rock that drew heavily from the same artistic wells as songwriting peers such as Emmylou Harris and Jackson Browne (whose album *Hold Out* topped the album chart for a week in 1980) were part of a vibrant musical scene based in Los Angeles in the first half of the seventies.[20] The Eagles reached a turning point with *Hotel California* (1976), a hard-edged concept album about social decadence that remains one of the best-selling albums of all time. In late 1979, before breaking up, the band released *The Long Run*, a suite of songs that included a series of hit singles—"Heartbreak Tonight," "The Long Run," and "I Can't Tell You Why." *The Long Run* was the second-best seller of the year for 1980 (after Pink Floyd's *The Wall*, to be discussed later).

Ronstadt was a true musical chameleon, though this wouldn't be fully apparent until later in the eighties. A Chicana with German ancestry, she had her first hit in 1967 with "Different Drum," a song written by Monkees star Mike Nesmith that she recorded with her band at the time, the Stone Poneys. In the mid-seventies, Ronstadt became a Nashville darling with hits like "Silver Threads and Golden Needles" (1973), "When Will I Be Loved" (1974), and her gorgeous remake of the Roy Orbison's "Blue Bayou" (1977). Actually, Ronstadt's signal skill as a hitmaker—beyond, of course, the power and beauty of her voice—was her exceptional taste in material, evident in her decision to interpret songs stretching from Tin Pan Alley (Oscar Hammerstein II's "When I Grow Too Old to Dream") to punk rock (Elvis Costello's "Alison"). Nineteen-eighty found Ronstadt at the end of the rock phase of her career with her album *Mad Love*, which tapped into the new wave in a string of hits that included "How Do I Make You," "Hurt So Bad," and "I Can't Let Go." Before the decade was over, she would be recording cantina music, collaborating with Frank Sinatra arranger Nelson Riddle, and appearing in the Gilbert and Sullivan opera *The Pirates of Penzance*.

Yet another good example of an established artist who commanded broad appeal across genres in 1980 was Stevie Wonder. Wonder, like Michael Jackson, was a child prodigy when he had his first hit on Motown in 1963 with "Fingertips (Part II)." He was a versatile team player for the label (cowriting, for example, the classic "Tears of a Clown" for Smokey Robinson and the Miracles) before taking charge of his career as an adult solo artist with a string of acclaimed albums that included *Innervisions* (1973) and *Songs from the Key of Life* (1976) as well as chart-topping pop classics like "Superstition" (1972), "You

Are the Sunshine of My Life" (1973) and "I Wish" (1976). In an indication of his interracial appeal—and a powerful instinct toward musical bridge-building—he also toured with the Rolling Stones. In 1980, Wonder released *Hotter than July*, which featured "Master Blaster (Jammin')" his joyful homage to Bob Marley. The album also featured "Happy Birthday," a tribute to Martin Luther King Jr. that was soon enlisted in the successful effort to turn MLK's birthday into a national holiday. Wonder continued to score hits into the eighties, but his artistic power waned (he did hit number one again in 1984 with the treacly "I Just Called to Say I Love You"). But he remains a bright light in the history of American popular music.

The commercial citadel of the popular music in 1980 remained rock and roll—or, in its shorthand formulation, rock. Mainstream rock act reputations were generated by touring, which built audiences that justified recording an album. (Record companies advanced money for both, and bands had to sell a lot of records to earn that money back and break into the black.) Once a critical mass of attention had been achieved, successful rock acts could run for decades on the strength of a core audience, usually white, and male, supplemented by occasional hits to give them currency with the wider public.

Rock was a kingdom of many mansions. We have already seen, for instance, how the subgenre of punk rock carved out a scene, established a set of premiere practitioners, and then proceeded to exert an influence far beyond its immediate fan base. Another such genre (one that long preceded punk, and has survived ever since) is hard rock, along with its principal variant, heavy metal, in which hard-driving electric guitars and shrieking vocals formed the core. The premier metal bands circa 1980—Black Sabbath, Judas Priest, Iron Maiden—forged deep, durable, and lucrative bonds with their audiences, mostly ignored by critics and FM radio stations. These bands operated almost entirely on a visceral level. At the other end of the metal spectrum—hard rock with more artistic ambition—was the Canadian power trio Rush, which wrote highly literate songs about free will, the French Revolution, and an Orwellian allegory of trees competing in a forest. (The whiff of Ayn Rand in songs like "Free Will" also suggested a tilt toward the coming neocon dispensation.) The band's 1980 album *Permanent Waves* led off with "The Spirit of Radio," a deeply affectionate tribute to the medium ("invisible airwaves crackle with life / bright antennae bristle with the energy") that fused emotion and intelligence.

There were also heavy metal records that crossed over into wide-release commercial success. The best example from 1980 was *Back in Black*, the highly acclaimed album by the Australian heavy metal band AC/DC. The group, which formed in Sydney in the early seventies, suffered a setback with the alcohol-related death of lead singer Bon Scott during the recording of the album, though he was capably replaced by new vocalist Brian Johnson. AC/DC also featured the distinctively crunching, minimalist style of guitarist Angus Young, who made a gimmick of wearing prep-school clothes on stage. The lead single from *Back in Black*, "You Shook Me All Night Long," only touched the bottom of the *Billboard* Top 40 in the fall of 1980, but has become among the most recognizable rock songs of all time. The album itself sold over 50 million copies.[21]

One heavy metal outfit built for pop success from the outset was Van Halen. Since the time of its now-classic debut album in 1978, the band—which consisted of brothers Eddie (guitar) and Alex (drums), Michael Anthony (bass), and the flamboyant front man David Lee Roth—racked up a string of hit singles that included a remake of the 1964 Kinks classic "You Really Got Me" (1978) and their own "Dance the Night Away" (1979). In 1980 Van Halen released its third album, *Women and Children First*, which, while not generating any hit singles, nevertheless kept the band foregrounded in the public eye. In years to come, Van Halen would be notable for its ability to mix inventive cover versions of classic songs (like its 1982 version of Martha and the Vandellas' 1964 Motown rave "Dancing in the Street") with memorable originals like "Jump," a number one song in 1984. Eddie Van Halen, of course, would perform the famous guitar solo for Michael Jackson's monster hit "Beat It," which topped the charts in 1983.

Another notable hard rocker who emerged into prominence in 1980 was a rare female artist, Pat Benatar. The daughter of a sheet-metal worker and a beautician, Benatar grew up on Long Island and considered a career in classical music before deciding to devote herself to rock. Her debut album, *In the Heat of the Night*, was released in 1979 and generated her first hit, "Heartbreaker." She then went on to release the signature song of her career "Hit Me with Your Best Shot" in the fall of 1980, the lead single from her album *Crimes of Passion*. Benatar became a prominent fixture of pop radio in the eighties, known for more musically nuanced hits, such as "Love Is a Battlefield" (1983) and "We Belong" (1984).

The preeminent female artists in heavy metal well before and after 1980 were sisters Ann and Nancy Wilson of Heart. The Seattle-based band was strongly influenced by Led Zeppelin, and indeed often performed a fine rendition of that band's classic "Rock & Roll." Heart also enjoyed a steady run of success on the pop chart that included the FM staple "Magic Man" in 1976 and the sharply metallic pop hit "Barracuda" in 1977. In 1980 the band released *Bebe Le Strange*, another strong outing that included a top-ten cover version of the Neville Brothers' 1966 hit "Tell It Like It Is." Heart went into commercial eclipse in the first half of the 1980s, but reemerged with a lighter pop sound that leaned more on synthesizers in the second half of the decade, enjoying success on the music-video circuit.

The regnant core of rock and roll in 1980 consisted of a series of veteran acts who commanded large audiences as a matter of course. In this realm, Britannia continued to rule. The best-selling album of 1980, which spent over three months at number one, was Pink Floyd's *The Wall*. (One of their previous albums, *Dark Side of the Moon*, holds the record for the longest continuous run on the *Billboard* album chart—almost fifteen years.) *The Wall* was a heavy-handed concept album of Dickensian oppression marked by maundering lyrics by chief songwriter Roger Waters, though guitarist David Gilmour is rightly considered a guitar legend, as evidenced by towering solos on songs like "Comfortably Numb." One track from the album, "Another Brick in the Wall (Part II)," also topped the pop charts in February 1980. This was a bit unusual, because traditional rock groups and their fans often ignored, even disdained, hit singles. This was true, for example, of Led Zeppelin, a band that enjoyed a top ten album for the year in 1980 with its swan song, *In Through the Out Door* (like *The Wall*, it too was released in late 1979). Though considered a minor work in the band's corpus, it soon found a devoted following inclined to acquire, and embrace, the band's body of work as a whole.

The hoariest of active British veterans on the 1980 rock landscape were the Rolling Stones. Often proclaimed "the greatest rock band in the world" since the breakup of The Beatles, the Stones had faded somewhat until the release of their 1978 album *Some Girls*, widely considered a highlight of the band's career. The Stones followed it up in the summer of 1980 with *Emotional Rescue*, which, while not as artistically successful, did generate a pair of hits in the title track and "She's So Cold."

Not all Brits were living off accumulated cultural capital in these years. In 1980, the ever-inventive David Bowie was making another musical pivot. Bowie had spent the late seventies in Berlin, drying out from drug addiction and recording a trilogy of acclaimed records—*Low* (1977), *Heroes* (1977), and *Lodger* (1979). *Heroes* was especially notable for its title track, which captured the moody, synth-driven tenor of Bowie's work, and a masterpiece in capturing a hard-bitten sense of antiheroic dignity that characterized the best music of the rock era. With *Scary Monsters (and Super Creeps)* in 1980, Bowie tacked back toward a tighter, more punchy direction with songs like "Ashes to Ashes"—in which he revisits the astronaut character from his 1969 hit "Space Oddity"—and "Fashion," redolent of his 1975 hit "Fame." In retrospect, *Scary Monsters* was a transition toward *Let's Dance*, his 1983 album that spawned a series of hits and turned Bowie into a bona fide pop star. Almost inevitably, it was produced by Nile Rodgers.[22]

No British act—for that matter, no act in popular music—was more exquisitely poised on the fulcrum between the seventies and eighties than Queen was in 1980. (Bowie teamed up with Queen the following year to record "Under Pressure," a highlight of both acts' careers.) The London-based quartet spent the seventies building a mass following as a rock band with both literal and figurative operatic flourishes, evident in songs like "Bohemian Rhapsody" from a *Night at the Opera* (1975) and "Somebody to Love" from *A Day at the Races* (1976). Queen's 1977 album *News of the World* included its global smash "We Will Rock You/We Are the Champions," which cemented the band as pop hitmakers stateside. Queen fully broke through in 1980 with its album *The Game*, which featured two number one songs that sit at either side of the decade divide.

The first, "Another One Bites the Dust," is surely the greatest disco song ever recorded by a non-disco act. It was written by Queen bassist John Deacon, who spent time hanging out in a studio with Nile Rodgers—it is truly astonishing how omnipresent Rodgers was in 1980—and forged a hook line, one that has been sampled countless times, straight out of the Chic playbook.[23] "Another One Bites the Dust" might not have ever been released had it not been for Michael Jackson, a Queen fan who often attended the band's shows. It was Jackson who told Queen lead vocalist Freddie Mercury that "you need a song the cats can dance to."[24] "Another One Bites the Dust" spent three weeks at number one and remains among the most recognizable songs of the era.

Queen's other chart-topper from *The Game* was "Crazy Little Thing Called Love," a straightforward rockabilly tune, complete with plucky guitars and heavy reverb, that's clearly an act of homage to Elvis Presley. Mercury and the band, whose stage personae could be positively baroque, adopted a stripped-down look marked by white T-shirts and black leather jackets in the visuals accompanying the song, indicative of an emerging trend toward a neoclassic sensibility in pop music. It is one that John Lennon picked up on in "(Just Like) Starting Over," and indeed became the very musical premise of The Stray Cats, a band formed in 1979 that enjoyed much success recording retro-minded original songs in the early eighties.

Other transitions to the new order were choppier. In the late 1970s, the ever-iconoclastic Bob Dylan did something even more shocking than his legendary appearance playing electric instruments at the Newport Folk Festival in 1965: he converted to evangelical Christianity. (That Dylan, born Robert Alan Zimmerman, the grandchild of Russian Jewish immigrants escaping pogroms, would do this makes it all the more striking.) In 1978, Dylan released *Slow Train Coming*, featuring the single "Gotta Serve Somebody," which actually landed in the middle of the *Billboard* Top 40. He followed it in 1980 with *Saved*, another collection of avowedly religious songs that was poorly received, no doubt in part because of the decidedly secular cast of critics and audiences. Few observers consider this period to be a highlight of Dylan's career, though the third album of this trilogy, *Shot of Love* (1981), produced a genuine masterpiece with "Every Grain of Sand" (movingly covered by Emmylou Harris on her 1995 landmark album, *Wrecking Ball*). If nothing else, this phase of Dylan's career showed him, once again, ahead of the curve as to where pop culture was heading.

And then there were those who were downright tetchy. One figure at the very center of pop music in 1980 was hitmaker Billy Joel. Joel had first emerged as a singer-songwriter of first rank with his 1973 ballad "Piano Man," which has long since passed into the pop music canon. He scored a major breakthrough with his 1977 album *The Stranger*, which generated no less than four top-twenty hits: "Just the Way You Are," "Movin' Out," "Only the Good Die Young," and "She's Always a Woman" (this kind of multihit performance was not routine until the mid-eighties, when albums like *Thriller* and *Purple Rain* did so). Similarly successful was Joel's 1978 follow-up, *52nd Street*, which included "My Life," "Big Shot," and "Honesty."

Joel was an exceptionally versatile pianist and gifted musical mimic with a unique feel for the musical center in these years, but his catchiness and lyricism were also accompanied by an underlying belligerence—a weird combination—that could grate. All these traits were apparent in his 1980 album *Glass Houses*, yet another multihit record that became the fourth best-selling album of the year. Here the piano man shifted gears to more of a guitar-based sound. In the chart-topping hit "It's Still Rock and Roll to Me," Joel rebels against the rebels of punk rock. "Everybody's talking 'bout the new sound / funny it's still rock and roll to me," he sneers in the chorus. "You May Be Right" revels in its narrator's obnoxiousness; "Sometimes a Fantasy" is a brash ode to masturbation. And yet the album also includes the deft "Don't Ask Me Why," whose delicate Latin stylings showcase Joel's musical sophistication. Joel remained one of the most reliable hitmakers in pop music until his self-imposed recording retirement in 1993, though he continued to perform live in a long-running residency at Madison Square Garden.

Its commercial success notwithstanding, *Glass Houses* was not among Joel's best outings—that honor probably belongs to his suburban concept album *The Nylon Curtain* from 1982, or his 1983 album *An Innocent Man*, which paid homage to Motown and his other musical influences. An undeniably inventive tunesmith, Joel's encyclopedic knowledge of pop idioms and his neoclassic sensibility were really closer to Tin Pan Alley than rock and roll. And this may be why he was so successful in the years on either side of 1980: he was a quintessential nostalgist at a time when many Americans were looking forward to looking back.

Bruce Springsteen was performing live with his fabled E Street Band in Philadelphia on December 8, 1980, the night John Lennon was shot by a crazed fan. Staff members backstage decided not to tell him until after the show was over. On December 9, Springsteen's bandmate Steven Van Zandt was surprised to learn that evening's show would still go on—he didn't think it should, and told Springsteen so. As he related to *Rolling Stone* soon after the event, Van Zandt remembered Springsteen replying to the effect of, "'This is what John Lennon inspired us to do and now it's our job to do the same thing for these other people, that today it was Lennon and tomorrow it might be me, and if it is. . . .' That's how he does every show, like it was his last. He lives every minute like it was his last. That's the way to live. It's really lucky to be close to him at moments like that."[25]

Lennon, for his part, had taken note of Springsteen, whose work he admired. On the night he died, "(Just Like) Starting Over" was sharing the top ten with Springsteen's first hit single, "Hungry Heart." Hours before he was shot, Lennon told an interviewer that it was his favorite song on the radio. He also expressed concern that Springsteen might find himself a victim of the kind of oppressive scrutiny

HUNGRY HEART

FIGURE 9. Bruce Springsteen at the time of *The River*. The ambitious album, a kaleidoscopic combination of raucous songs interspersed with others of vertiginous depth, consolidated his claim as the greatest rock star of his generation—but one who would prove to be more of a loyal son than a founding father. (Photofest)

Lennon himself had experienced. "God help Bruce Springsteen when they decide he's no longer God," he told veteran music journalist Jonathan Cott on December 5. "I haven't seen him, but I've heard such good things about him. Right now his fans are happy. He's told them about being drunk and chasing girls and cars and everything, and that's about the level they enjoy. But when he gets down to facing his own success and growing older and having to produce it again and again, they'll turn on him, and I hope he survives it."[26]

But that reckoning never happened. Lennon was correct that Springsteen's music had evolved significantly since his early work, which had been marked by carefree youthful abandon in songs like "Blinded by the Light"—which Manfred Mann's Earth Band had taken to number one in an idiosyncratic version of the song in 1976— and his epic dazzler "Rosalita." Like Lennon once had, Springsteen also moved in a decidedly more adult direction, especially since the release of *Born to Run* in 1975 (the song of the same name had grazed the bottom of the Top 20 that year). But while Lennon had restlessly moved away from his working-class roots and plunged into musical experimentation, Springsteen had instead hewed much closer to the world that made him, forging a bond with his audience that has since become the stuff of legend. If Lennon was Beethoven, Springsteen was Brahms, the dutiful son of the rock rebellion, one who lovingly evoked, borrowed, and even resurrected his influences. The backup singers of "Hungry Heart" are Mark Volman and Howard Kaylan of the Turtles, the pop band best known for their 1967 hit "Happy Together."

"Hungry Heart" was the lead single from Springsteen's 1980 album *The River*, a record that is perhaps the purest specimen of its kind in capturing the essence of popular culture that year. The album was a two-disc set in which he self-consciously tried to juxtapose his raucous rock songs alongside his more meditative ones—a compression Springsteen achieved in the musically effervescent "Hungry Heart" itself, with unbroken lines like "We fell in love I knew it had to end." So it is, for example, that his Dostoevskian masterpiece "Stolen Car," about a criminal who longs to get caught, is followed by "Ramrod," a paean to street racing culture. And yet in its willful anachronism, Springsteen has characterized "Ramrod" as "one of the saddest I've written."[27] The album is stuffed with snapshots of a receding industrial-worker vision of life, ranging from the joyous innocence of the dockworker in "Out in the Street" to the dreamily dated suitor of "I Wanna Marry You." The back cover of the album depicts a storefront window of a wedding party as a set of cardboard figures, reflecting Springsteen's desire to endow the most ordinary, even hackneyed, symbols with transcendental power.[28]

Make no mistake: Springsteen's fundamental conservative *cultural* impulses were not necessarily *political* ones. On November 5, 1980, a month before that Philadelphia show and the night after Ronald Reagan was elected president, Springsteen was at Arizona State University. "I don't know what you thought about what happened last night," he told the crowd, "but I thought it was pretty terrifying."[29] He then launched into "Badlands," the leadoff track from his 1978 album *Darkness on the Edge of Town*, a song about frustrated, but still living, dreams. Though he was circumspect about his political views for most of his career, there is little question that Springsteen saw himself as a man of the Left.

But it was in many ways an old Left. Springsteen was at heart always a conservative in his musical tastes, but the values he sought to conserve were different ones than those embraced by Reagan. Similarly, he was always a patriot at heart, but what he loved about America could never be reduced to a flag or a slogan, or entirely free of sorrow even as he refused to surrender hope. His music was dedicated to the proposition that, for better and worse, this land was *our* land.

SHOT OF J.R.

FIGURE 10. Larry Hagman as the infamous J.R. Ewing in the hit TV series *Dallas* (1978–1991). The show topped the ratings in 1980, in large measure for the national mania surrounding the identity of his attempted murderer at the end of the show's third season. "I don't suppose you could tell me who shot J.R.," Queen Elizabeth II asked Hagman on a royal visit that summer. "No ma'am, not even for you," Hagman replied. (Photofest)

CHAPTER 5

Ebb and Flow

Tidal Shifts in Broadcast Television

W HO SHOT J.R.?
That was the question. Actually, that was *the* question—more than the outcome of the presidential election; more than who was going to win any given championship; more than any celebrity marriage, breakup, or any other life event—in 1980. It was the question that made *Dallas* the number one television show that year. It remained unanswered for a full eight months between the finale of the show's third season in March 1980 and its resolution that November, four episodes into its fourth. The shooter was finally disclosed—naturally, during the so-called sweeps season, when viewership numbers helped determine advertising rates for the coming months—in what became the most watched TV episode of all time.[1]

Certainly, there were plenty of candidates for would-be killers of J.R., played with great panache by Larry Hagman as the man millions loved to hate. The masterfully executed cliffhanger episode, "A House Divided," provided any number of plausible candidates: Was it his alcoholic wife Sue Ellen (Linda Gray), who he was planning on committing to a sanitarium against her will? His sister-in-law Kristin (Mary Crosby), who was trying to steal him away from Sue Ellen but who J.R. had just dumped? His banker Vaughn Leland (Dennis Patrick), one of a number of business associates to whom J.R. sold foreign oil leases days before they were nationalized in an unnamed

Asian country? His former henchman Alan Beam (Randolph Powell), who J.R. framed for rape? There was also the usual standby, Cliff Barnes (Ken Kercheval), part of an intergenerational family feud, whom J.R. had just cheated out of millions. The episode ends with two shots in the dark and J.R. writhing on the floor of his office; viewers had a summer of reruns, and countless conversations, to speculate on what came next. Actually, it was not clear whether J.R. would live or die, in part because Hagman was holding out for more money and his return was in doubt. (His gambit paid off handsomely, and indeed he was the only actor to appear in each of the show's 357 episodes.) The identity of the shooter—at least three different endings were shot—was also a tightly kept secret. "I don't suppose you could tell me who shot J.R.," Queen Elizabeth II asked Hagman on a royal visit that summer (he lived much of the time in England, and *Dallas* was very popular abroad). "No ma'am, not even for you," Hagman replied. Vendors at the Republican National Convention in August sold a button that read A DEMOCRAT SHOT J.R."[2]

It was far from clear that *Dallas* would ever become a global phenomenon when it first aired as something of an experiment in 1978. Television writer David Jacobs, who was under contract with production company Lorimar, had developed an idea for a series about a set of couples living in a suburban cul-de-sac that he called *Knots Landing*, which he pitched to CBS. The network was not interested in that idea, but it saw possibilities in a family saga on a somewhat grander scale. For Jacobs, a saga meant Texas—a state he had driven through once, quickly. Literally overnight, he came up with a concept about a clan in the oil business in Houston. One of his collaborators impulsively shifted the location to Dallas, which had more cultural caché— "extravagant, but not ostentatious," as Jacobs later explained the sensibility as he came to understand it, something that would make more sense as the show spawned a series of gaudier imitators.[3] The network agreed to back a five-episode miniseries as a trial run for the show (this was later considered its first season), which was followed by a full order of a twenty-four-episode second season. By the third, the show was a hit, and by the fourth it became a bona fide phenomenon. *Dallas* ultimately ran for fourteen seasons until 1991, a television personification of what the eighties would be all about.

The point of departure for the series was Bobby Ewing (Patrick Duffy), the youngest of three sons of Ellie (Barbara Bel Geddes) and Jock Ewing (Jim Davis). Bobby married Pamela Barnes (Victoria Principal), daughter of Digger Barnes (played by a number of actors, notably the veteran Keenan Wynn.) Jock and Digger had been partners in the oil business in the thirties until a dispute between them ended their friendship as the Ewing clan began its meteoric rise. It didn't help matters that Digger had also been a suitor for Ellie's affection; she was the daughter of a wealthy cattle rancher. The middle Ewing brother, Gary (Ted Shackleford), was the black sheep of the family and had fled the family's Southfork Ranch years earlier, leaving behind his daughter Lucy (Charlene Tilton), raised by her grandparents and an all too worldly adolescent as the saga began. The scion of the Ewing clan was J.R., who at the series outset had just taken over the Ewing drilling empire from his semiretired father.

The original intention of Jacobs and his collaborators was that Bobby would be the hero. Actually, the early episodes were dominated by Pamela, a strong-minded woman who repeatedly outwitted J.R.'s venial schemes. "Women don't exist for men. We exist for ourselves first," she told J.R.'s wife Sue Ellen in a typical line (this one from the 1979 episode "Mastectomy, Part 2"; Ellie had to have one). "Not if you're married to a Ewing," Sue Ellen replied. "I *am* married to a Ewing," was Pamela's riposte, even as she made clear that her marital status was secondary to her feminism. Pamela's professional aspirations in the fashion business would be an ongoing source of tension between her and the kindly, if less enlightened, Bobby.

As a matter of genre, *Dallas*—with its endless plots of overlapping family intrigue extending over multiple episodes—fell into the realm of the much beloved, and largely female, television genre: the soap opera, shows in which women's concerns were central. These dramas had long been a staple of daytime television. The genre was enjoying a revival of sorts in 1980, when the long-running soap *General Hospital* (1963–) was running its famous "Luke and Laura" plot that would end in a much-watched wedding in 1981. In revving the genre up with much higher production values and giving the show a marquee prime time slot on a weekly rather than daily basis, *Dallas* emerged as a cultural hybrid with a strong demographic base.

The character of J.R. widened that base. Some of this is simply a matter of the psychic logic of storytelling—villains are usually more interesting than heroes, and J.R's masculine swagger held appeal for both men and women. Some too, as indicated, is a matter of the actor who portrayed him. Hagman, son of screen legend Mary Martin, was a native Texan who had first come to national attention as a straight man in the hit sitcom *I Dream of Jeannie* (1965–1970), in which he played Major Anthony Nelson, an astronaut who suddenly finds himself living with a woman of magical powers who sows chaos in his life. (His costar, Barbara Eden, appeared with him in a string of 1990 episodes of *Dallas* in which she plays a vengeful billionaire.) But J.R. was a role of another order. As TV critic Kimberly Potts explained in a 2020 appreciation of the series, "Larry Hagman became the defining *Dallas* star," noting the "unabashed glee" with which his character engaged in his dastardly acts. "Every episode of *Dallas* ends with a trademark freeze frame, and many of those are close-ups of a grinning J.R., just after he's double-crossed a business associate or driven his long-suffering alcoholic wife Sue Ellen to another sanitarium stay. The charm Hagman wrings out of uttering one 'Darlin' is worth both of those Emmys he was nominated for."[4]

But the appeal of J.R. specifically, and *Dallas* more generally, has broader cultural significance. The show debuted during the Texas oil boom of the seventies, an era when the state's truculent swagger stood in sharp contrast to a Rust Belt staggering under the weight of the era's energy crisis. (Remember that 1980 was the year of *Urban Cowboy* and its blockbuster soundtrack—the Lone Star State was clearly having a moment.) While Texas would endure a harsh hangover when prices crashed in the eighties, its much-touted free-market entrepreneurial style was well suited to the shifting winds of the new decade. J.R. was often the voice of this economic libertarianism. "Oh, the tax revolt is sure shakin' the politicians up—I just love it," he says in a typical early line, this one from the 1978 episode "Reunion, Part 2." There can be no doubt who he voted for in the presidential election of 1980.

Viewers, for their part, were casting their figurative ballots for *Dallas* in the all-important currency of ratings. After its tentative beginnings on at 10 p.m. on Sunday nights in the show's first season, *Dallas* reached number six for the 1979–80 season, when it moved to the much higher profile slot of Friday nights. It was the highest-rated show of the 1980–81 season, with viewership reaching tens of millions weekly. The 1980 episode "Who Done It?"—to avoid spoilers, the killer will be identified by footnote[5]—was watched by over 80 million viewers domestically and over three-quarters of all people watching television that night, to say nothing of a global audience for whom the show became a byword for American culture. The show remained in first or second place through 1985.

Dallas, then, was an artifact of its time. But while it was at the leading edge of cultural change, the show was nevertheless embedded in a television shoreline marked by ebb and flow.

Living in a time when anything we might want to watch, hear, or read is literally at our fingertips, it may be hard to remember—or realize—that for most of recorded history, cherished cultural documents were limited in their availability. This is especially true of television shows. A typical TV program was broadcast at a set time once a week, and a given episode would run in the fall and be aired again, or rerun, once in the spring. After a few years, a really successful show would move from a major national network—there were three: CBS, NBC, and ABC—into syndication on local TV stations, where it might run weekdays, Monday to Friday, "stripped" into a daily time slot. But achieving this level of success was a generally unpredictable business, both in terms of how long such a network run might last and how likely you would be able to see a given episode. This is one reason why most shows had plots that were compartmentalized, so you could figure out what was going on (or what you had forgotten), whenever you happened to catch it.

By 1980 television had been the dominant cultural medium in American life for about a quarter of a century. Its debut in the fifties had been a source of wonder; in endless social commentary, TV was considered an embodiment of as well as an agent of modernity itself. Television was alternately hailed as a transformative medium that informed and enlightened, or condemned as a dangerous drug that addled and numbed. Either way, it consumed large amounts of discretionary time: by 1980 the average American watched about seven hours a day.[6] Those hours were of different kinds, including morning shows, after-school programming, late night, and, of course, the showcase of prime time, whose heart was 8–11 p.m., which is the focus of the discussion here.

In these years—the years when television broadcasting was at its mature peak, just as it was beginning to splinter with the rise of cable television and before the arrival of the internet—the crucial factor in whether a show would succeed or fail came down to its place on the network schedule, and, to a growing extent, *which* people watched, as some demographics were more valuable than others. There were two axes in this programming matrix. The first was where a given show might be internally: what night it ran, what time it ran, and what preceded or followed it on its network. The other was external: which shows it was competing against at the same night and time, and how it compared with other shows of its genre. Success or failure was not necessarily a matter of head-to-head matchups; some shows cost more to make than others, for example, and some could command higher or lower advertising rates based on their demographics, which were becoming increasingly important. A half-hour show typically allotted about five minutes for ads, and a one-hour show about ten. A program with anemic ratings might not get canceled right away—it might get a chance to grow, for example, or be moved to a more propitious slot in the hopes it would catch on—but sooner or later, every show had to carry its own weight in terms of commanding adequate advertising dollars to justify its cost.

The network executives who made these decisions were sometimes accorded the status of Svengalis. Fred Silverman—dubbed "the man with the golden gut" by *Time* magazine[7]—started his career at CBS and became a household name as the architect of ABC's prime-time dominance for much of the late seventies. (He had less success during a stint at NBC in the eighties.) He and peers like Robert Daly at CBS and Brandon Tartikoff at NBC pored over data and schedules in the quest to deploy assets in ways that maximized what was essentially a guessing game. There were times that a strategic tweak could get demonstrable results. One good example was the hit series *M*A*S*H* (1972–1983), about medics during the Korean War. Its early ratings were shaky when the show was first broadcast on Sunday nights. But when it was embedded in a CBS Saturday night schedule that included *All in the Family* (1971–1979), *The Mary Tyler Moore Show* (1970–1977), *The Bob Newhart Show* (1972–1978), and *The Carol Burnett Show* (1967–1978)—a lineup that can be usefully compared with that of the legendary 1927 New York Yankees—*M*A*S*H* emerged as a durable and profitable mainstay for CBS. It was then moved to Monday nights, where it became a lead-in for other shows trying to get a purchase on the network schedule. *M*A*S*H* was the number four show in the 1980–1981 season.[8] It also spawned the successful spinoff *Trapper John, M.D.* (1979–1986).

Dallas may have been at the leading edge of where television culture was headed in 1980, but many holdovers from the seventies, considered a golden age by TV critics, were still going strong. Among the most important were the sitcoms of Norman Lear, perhaps the most powerful producer in the history of television. Lear was the driving force behind *All in the Family*, which was the number one show for five years running in the mid-seventies and spawned a series of spinoffs. The sitcom's run concluded in 1979, but its star, Carroll O'Connor, got his own vehicle in *Archie Bunker's Place* (1979–1983), set in the bar where the working-class stiff finally graduated to small businessman. *Archie Bunker's Place* finished eleventh in the ratings in 1979–1980 and thirteenth in 1980–1981.

Another *All in the Family* spinoff—this one even more durable and almost as successful—was *The Jeffersons* (1975–1985). Louise and George Jefferson (Isabel Sanford and Sherman Hemsley) were neighbors of the Bunker family whose success in the dry-cleaning business led them to buy an apartment on Park Avenue, where they jostled with a gallery of diverse characters. *The Jeffersons*, whose family name is clearly meant to constitute ironic homage to the Founding Father, was a landmark in television history not simply as a portrayal of black life, but more specifically *affluent* black life, adding an important class dimension to the popular discourse at a time when millions of white Americans were only beginning to achieve any sense of nuance in their understanding of African Americans. *The Jeffersons* was firmly ensconced as a top ten show in the years on either side of 1980.

The Lear empire also continued portraying the realities of working women's lives. *One Day at a Time* (1975–1984) featured Bonnie Franklin as a divorcée raising two adolescent daughters (Mackenzie Phillips and Valerie Bertinelli) in Indianapolis. The show tackled parent–child relationships, career concerns, and the romantic challenges facing middle-aged women. It lasted nine seasons, clustered alongside *The Jeffersons* and *Archie Bunker's Place* in or near the top ten circa 1980.

One other notably female and working-class-centered show from this period is *Alice* (1976–1985). Based on the 1974 Martin Scorsese film *Alice Doesn't Live Here Anymore*, in which a young widowed mother—Ellen Burstyn won an Oscar for her performance in the role—becomes a waitress in the process of trying to forge a new life as a singer. Alice in the series was played by Linda Lavin; Vic Tayback reprised his role as Mel, the owner of the diner where she worked. Another key character was the salty-tongued Flo (Diane Ladd in the film; Polly Holliday in the show) who became famous for her tart one-liners, notably "Kiss my grits!" Flo went on to get a spinoff in her own name in 1980, which prospered briefly before it was canceled in 1981. *Alice* remained a top ten show into the eighties.

Most of the shows discussed here were sitcoms, and most of them originated in the first half of the seventies, even as they lasted well into the eighties. One reason so many of them were highly regarded is that they weaved social and political concerns into the fabric of their storylines. This was true of yet another early seventies holdover, *The Waltons*, a sometimes sentimental but liberal-minded rural family drama set during the Great Depression. By 1980, *The Waltons*, whose plots by that time centered on World War II, was fraying in quality, in no small measure due to the loss of key cast members like Richard Thomas, who played John-Boy, the aspiring writer whose perspective framed each episode. But the show's presence in the prime-time schedule was an important indication that cultural change can be a slow and overlapping process as once-popular sensibilities recede and new ones emerge to take their place.

New television programming in the second half of the seventies, by contrast, was marked by a decidedly different tone. There were two divergent strands that emerged in this period. One was a trend toward more broadly satirical (and often sexual) humor that pushed the limits of what was still a conservative medium that depended on advertisers nervous about any content that might offend potential customers. The other was a new nostalgia that prefigured the cultural conservatism that would come to define the eighties. In a way, these were two sides of the same coin, each reflecting a restlessness with the social reform ethos of the sixties.

The pioneer in terms of a new cultural iconoclasm was *Saturday Night Live*, which made its debut in 1975. Although it was experienced as a programming novelty—particularly in terms of scheduling a high-profile show in the broadcasting graveyard of 11:30 p.m. on Saturday night—*SNL*'s formula of sketch comedy and live musical performances dated back to the very origins of the medium, when programs like *Your Show of Shows* (1950–1954) helped define what TV would actually look and sound like. What was different was a snarky, knowing, sometimes absurdist edge (the Killer Bees skits; Dan Ackroyd's bloody satire of Julia Child bleeding to death in her kitchen; Gilda Radner's famed TV commentator Roseanne Roseannadanna) that went beyond earlier relatively subversive humor like that of *The Smothers Brothers Comedy Hour* (1967–1969) or *Laugh-in* (1968–1973). By the end of the seventies, however, *SNL* had fallen on hard times. Its fifth season of 1979–1980 was the first without its cornerstone stars

of John Belushi and Ackroyd, and its sixth proceeded without producer Lorne Michaels, whose request for a sabbatical was denied and
he was in effect fired, leading most of the show's performers and writers to exit in protest. The show was redubbed *Saturday Night Live '80*,
and it was widely regarded as a flop (there were a couple of parodies of
Dallas that season, including one in which a cast member uttered an
ad-libbed forbidden expletive on the air, which led to mass firings).[9]
SNL gradually recovered its footing with the emergence of Eddie
Murphy and a new generation of talent in his wake; the show's future
was secured with the return of Michaels in 1985, where he has been
ever since. *SNL* is now a television institution.

The subversive edge, such as it was, of prime-time TV circa 1980
was pitched toward titillating viewers rather than intellectually
engaging them. Perhaps the most famous example of this was *Charlie's Angels* (1976–1981), a weekly drama that was in theory a feminist
statement—female private eyes battling sexist corruption—but was
really more of a showcase for eye candy in the form of its stars, which
is why it was one of a number of shows labeled "Jiggle TV." The true
phenom of the series was Farrah Fawcett, a former model who briefly
became a superstar; she left the show after its first season but made a
number of return appearances, including one in February 1980. Fawcett was clear about the source of the *Charlie's Angels* appeal: "When
the show was number three [in the weekly ratings], I thought it was
our acting," she told *TV Guide*. "When we got to be number one, I
decided it could only be because none of us wears a bra."[10] But by that
point *Charlie's Angels* had already begun its slide out of the Nielsen
annual top ten, and was eventually canceled before the end of its fifth
season. It spawned a series of sequels in the twenty-first century.

More durable was *Three's Company* (1977–1984), a sitcom laced
with double entendres. Based on the British series *Man about the
House, Three's Company* featured John Ritter as a young man sharing
a Santa Monica apartment with two women (Suzanne Somers and
Joyce DeWitt), an arrangement only possible because their nosy landlord (Norman Fell) wrongly believes he's gay. (Ritter, ironically, had
previously portrayed a prudish minister on multiple episodes of *The*

Waltons.) Somers's character was notably retrograde as the very embodiment of the dumb blonde, but such complaints, which were widespread, did not dent the show's appeal in these years, when it was frequently in the top three annually. A spinoff focusing on Fell's character and that of his libidinous wife, *The Ropers*, ran in 1979–1980.

The most wildly anarchic sitcom of the period, one that managed to be saturated with both innuendo and warmth, was *Mork and Mindy* (1978–1982). The show starred the prodigiously talented Robin Williams as an antic alien from outer space who makes a life with a young woman (Pam Dawber) in Boulder, Colorado. Williams outpaced the show's writers with his improvisations—and made it hard for Dawber to keep a straight face while shooting scripts.[11] *Mork and Mindy* exploded onto the network schedule and instantly became the number three show in its first season. Executives at ABC decided to leverage its success by counterprogramming the show against hit series from other networks, which damaged its ratings, and it may be that the show's sheer novelty wore off after the first couple seasons. *Mork and Mindy* was a fading meteor by 1980, but it was clear to all observers that Williams's career as an actor and comedian was only beginning. His first starring film, Robert Altman's *Popeye*, was released in December 1980 to mixed reviews and middling box office, but Williams went on to superstardom in the eighties with films *Good Morning, Vietnam* (1987) and *Dead Poets Society* (1989). Williams and Dawber reunited briefly when they appeared together in Williams's series *The Crazy Ones* (2013–2014) shortly before his tragic suicide.

Mork and Mindy entered the television schedule in the most unlikely of ways: as a spinoff from an episode of *Happy Days* (1974–1984), perhaps the most beloved sitcom of the era. *Happy Days* was the brainchild of producer Garry Marshall, who first came to prominence by developing *The Odd Couple* (1970–1975) based on the 1965 Neil Simon Broadway play and 1968 movie about a pair of mismatched roommates. Like Norman Lear, Marshall was a television impresario who enjoyed a string of successful shows in the seventies. But while Lear tried to push the envelope, Marshall peddled in nostalgia, which proved to be a powerful countercurrent to what in many ways was a decade of cultural transgression.

It was during the 1970s that the 1950s were rediscovered—and, in some quarters, celebrated—as a time of relative innocence in American society. The novelty act Sha Na Na performed golden oldies throughout the decade and hosted a variety show on TV from 1977 to 1981. Director George Lucas had his cinematic breakthrough in 1973 with *American Graffiti*, a loving re-creation of a memorable night in the Modesto, California, of his youth. ("Where were you in '62?" was the promotional line in the movie, but its setting harkened back to the Eisenhower years much more than to the sixties.) Another paean to the youthful fifties, the long-running musical *Grease*, made its debut on Broadway in 1971; it became a smash hit film in 1978, with a soundtrack that spawned a series of hits, among them ones sung by the two leads, Australian pop singer Olivia Newton-John, and superstar John Travolta, following up on his success in *Saturday Night Fever* the previous year.[12]

Happy Days began as an unsold pilot episode that ended up on the anthology series *Love, American Style* (1969–1974). It starred Ron Howard, whose TV stardom began with a child role on *The Andy Griffith Show* (1960–1968) now playing as an adolescent growing up in 1950s Milwaukee surrounded by a loving family and friends that included his mom (Marion Ross) and dad (Tom Bosley). George Lucas cast Howard in *American Graffiti* on the strength of that episode, and that in turn led ABC to pick up the series. After performing well in its initial season, *Happy Days* sagged in the ratings until Marshall decided to foreground its comic elements, greatly bolstered by the character of the leather-jacketed Fonzie (Henry Winkler), whose signature line "Aaaaay!" became a pop culture mainstay.[13] The show was the most popular in the country in 1976–1977. However, it is known among TV aficionados as the source of the phrase "jumping the shark," referring to "a defining moment [in a show] when you know from now on . . . it's all downhill . . . it will never be the same," in the words of the University of Michigan student Jon Hein, who coined it.[14] The episode in question was an absurd one from 1977 in which Fonzie goes to Hollywood and competes with a cocky local by waterskiing over a shark, marking a point where the character would increasingly dominate the show. Jumping the shark notwithstanding, *Happy Days* did not in fact decline from a ratings standpoint; it remained in the top twenty into the early eighties.

For a time, the *Happy Days* spinoff *Laverne & Shirley* (1976–1983), starring Marshall's sister Penny as the former and Cindy Williams as the latter, was even more popular, depicting the life of two young working-class women employed in a Milwaukee beer factory and parrying their clueless but amusing friends Lennie (Michael McKean) and Squiggy (David Lander), whose abrupt entrances were masterpieces of comic timing. (Their talent-show performance of their song "Night After Night" is one of the most hilariously clueless moments in the history of television, and foreshadows McKean's star turn in the classic 1984 film *This Is Spinal Tap*.)[15] *Happy Days* and *Laverne & Shirley* were shows about the fifties that were created in the seventies and continued to have a life into the eighties, demonstrating how the overlapping tides of history could coexist in a single moment.

Another exercise in nostalgia that was nearing its end as the eighties arrived was *Little House on the Prairie* (1974–1982). The show was based on the classic novels of Laura Ingalls Wilder—here we're talking about a seventies show based on 1930s novels about the 1870s—starring Melissa Gilbert as a girl growing up in rural Minnesota. The show spawned a series of sequels and remakes into the twenty-first century. It was the number ten show in 1980–1981.

Of course, not all successful TV shows circa 1980 were period pieces, and not all were scripted dramas or sitcoms. Nor did they all appear on broadcast television. Modern cable television was still in its infancy that year. Actually, cable TV dated back to the 1940s as a means of providing programming for people living in remote rural areas who lacked good reception. The idea that a cable station or network could present original content first took root in the 1960s for athletic events like boxing matches. It got taken one step further when Home Box Office (HBO), founded in 1972, began showing classic and recent movies. HBO was followed in rapid succession by a companion network, Cinemax, as well as by a host of competitors. Cable was also gradually becoming a platform for other kinds of programming, such as the Christian Broadcasting Network (CBN), which took advantage of the rising tide of evangelicalism in American culture.

One of the most notable developments in the history of cable TV occurred in 1980: the debut of the Cable News Network (CNN), launched by entrepreneur Ted Turner. Turner overcame skepticism that there really was a market for seven-day, twenty-four-hour news coverage, in the process changing the pace and tenor of American journalism. It would be a few years, however, before its impact would be fully evident.[16]

As a matter of fact, the top-rated show of 1979–1980 was a news program: 60 Minutes (1968–), created by producer Don Hewitt. It was modeled on a magazine format, which is to say a series of longform stories in each hourly installment—the show's stopwatch logo became a cover of sorts that listed volume and issue number. The program became the prototype for a style of sometimes confrontational investigative reporting whose hosts (initially Harry Reasoner and Mike Wallace) became stars in their own right. The show had a standing feature that included contrasting opinions, "Point/Counterpoint," famously lampooned by Dan Ackroyd and Jane Curtin on SNL, including Ackroyd's famous line, "Jane, you ignorant slut." Light humor was also featured on 60 Minutes, provided by Andy Rooney, though he later became controversial for alleged comments about blacks and documented comments against gay people.[17] In 1980, the show ran a Dan Rather interview probing whether sixty-nine-year-old Ronald Reagan was too old to be president, a profile of a wife and mother born without arms, and an exploration of the culture of Rastafarianism, suggesting the range it tried to cultivate.[18] Since 60 Minutes was a show whose stock and trade was the revelation of scandal, it seems only fair to note that the program itself was marked by long-standing habits of harassment on the part of its many (male) hosts and correspondents.[19] But a half-century later, the show is still running strong—forty years after topping the Nielsen ratings,

60 Minutes was again perched on top in 2020 with its coverage of COVID-19.[20]

In 1980, a magazine-style approach—short narratives embedded within a larger, ongoing storytelling vehicle—was applied to dramas as well. The prototype here was *The Love Boat* (1977–1984), produced by yet another television durably successful impresario, Aaron Spelling, known as a creator of shows stretching from *The Mod Squad* (1968-1973) to *Beverly Hills 90210* (1990-2000). *The Love Boat*, which peaked in popularity at number five in 1980, featured a cast of recurring regulars led by Captain Merrill Stubing (Gavin McLeod, who had a reliable supporting role in *The Mary Tyler Moore Show*) taking a series of cruise guests on a ship where they found love, worked out problems, or some combination of both. Those guests were often played by celebrities from other TV shows; the series was also a way-station for higher-profile careers. Tom Hanks made his TV debut in a 1980 episode of *The Love Boat*, just before taking a starring role in *Bosom Buddies,* a sitcom in which he and costar Peter Scolari played men who dressed as women in order to live in an affordable apartment building. That series premiered in November 1980 and ran for two seasons, serving as Hanks's springboard to superstardom.[21]

Another Spelling-produced magazine-style ABC drama that immediately followed *The Love Boat* in the network's successful Saturday night lineup was *Fantasy Island*. If the former was a voyage, *Fantasy Island* was a destination—a remote Pacific Island. The host of *Fantasy Island* was the elegant but enigmatic Mr. Roarke, played by Ricardo Montalbán, ably assisted by his associate Tattoo (Hervé Villechaize), who shouted "Ze plane! Ze plane!" to announce the arrival of guests in every episode, becoming a catchphrase. Those arrivals, who came from all walks of life, sometimes paying a fortune to do so, would have their dreams come true. But the results were often cautionary tales, as many characters found themselves dealing with more than they bargained for, sometimes requiring a timely rescue by Mr. Roarke (there was a supernatural overlay to some episodes). As with *The Love Boat*, which generally had stronger ratings, *Fantasy Island* was the basis of subsequent remakes of various kinds.

It was in 1979–1980 that another, quasi-magazine format genre of television show emerged—a forerunner of what we now know as reality television. *Real People* (1979–1984) debuted on NBC and landed in the top twenty at a time when the network was struggling to find a purchase in prime time. The show featured a series of hosts who appeared before a live studio audience and introduced taped pieces that featured ordinary Americans with unusual skills or jobs. *Real People* became the breakout vehicle for fitness guru Richard Simmons, who was featured in one episode of the show. "Some of you have small ones, and some of you have big ones, and it doesn't make any difference," he told his largely female clientele in a persona that combined candor, empathy, and self-help. "You want firm ones."[22] For the next two decades, Simmons rode a campy line between real and fictive personae to massive celebrity that combined acting, personal appearances, and a video empire centered on the fitness craze of the 1980s. Though he never disclosed his sexuality, Simmons exuded a gay vibe that he used to project a populist message that some found more approachable than other fitness stars of the time, such as Jane Fonda, whose exercise videos would also become a sensation in the eighties. His disappearance from public life in the 2010s spawned a high-profile Apple podcast *Missing Richard Simmons* in 2017–2018.

In 1980, ABC responded to *Real People* with a show of its own, *That's Incredible!*, which leaped to success as the third-most-watched show that year (though it settled much lower after that). *That's Incredible!* was less focused on occupations than stunts, reenactments, and technological breakthroughs. One 1980 episode, for example, featured a hang-gliding dog (the show spawned a spinoff, *Those Amazing Animals*, in 1980–1981). One other episode of note featured a five-year-old golfer named Eldrick "Tiger" Woods, who had already logged two years on the links before his appearance. There were, however, some who protested that the show's gimmicks put participants in unnecessary danger, like the person in the first season who unsuccessfully tried to catch a bullet with his teeth. A number of stunts did in fact result in accidents.[23] This proto-reality television trend was extended still further by ABC's resurrection of *Ripley's Believe It or Not*, which

NOBLE REDNECKS

FIGURE 11. Christopher Mayer (as Vance Duke) and Byron Cherry (as Coy Duke) in The *Dukes of Hazzard* (1979–1985), second in the ratings only to *Dallas* in 1980. Situated at the ideological crossroads between Jimmy Carter's Georgia and Ronald Reagan's Orange County, this hour-long CBS series, part of that network's successful effort to overtake ABC in the ratings sweepstakes, looked backward and forward at the same time. (Photofest)

began as a newspaper feature by illustrator Robert Ripley in the early twentieth century, was made into a series of books, became a radio show in the thirties, and then a TV show in the forties, before another revival series in 1982–1986. But reality TV as an established and diversifying genre would not really take off in the United States until the arrival of *Survivor* (2000–) and similar shows in the twenty-first century.

No show in 1980 captured the transitional zeitgeist of the time more vividly than the one perched at number two for the 1980–1981 season: *The Dukes of Hazzard* (1979–1985). Situated at the ideological crossroads between Jimmy Carter's Georgia and Ronald Reagan's Orange County, this hour-long CBS series, part of that network's successful effort to overtake ABC in the ratings sweepstakes, looked backward and forward at the same time.

The roots of *The Dukes of Hazzard* were in the 1975 movie *Moonrunners*, written and directed by Guy Waldron, who went on to develop the TV series. The film starred the weathered veteran Robert Mitchum and was based on the real-life exploits of whiskey moonshiner Jerry Rushing of Hazzard County, Kentucky (transferred to a fictive locale of the same name in Georgia).[24] Core cast members of the show were cousins Bo and Luke Duke (John Schneider and Tom Wopat, briefly replaced by Christopher Mayer and Byron Cherry), their cousin Daisy (Catherine Bach, whose cutoff denim shorts helped make her a sex symbol), and their uncle Jesse (Denver Pyle). Hazzard County is run by inept sheriff Rosco P. Coltrane (James Best), who works at the behest of the corrupt Jefferson Davis, or "Boss," Hogg (Sorrell Booke, who in a previous life worked as a counterintelligence agent during the Korean War).[25]

The Dukes of Hazzard took advantage of what might be termed "Georgia chic," a phenomenon in the late seventies that followed Carter's election to the presidency in 1976. There was, for example, the short-lived sitcom *Carter Country* (1977–1979), which starred Victor French as the police chief of the fictive small town of Clinton Corners, with Kene Holliday as his college-educated, city-bred, black deputy, as they deal with small-time racism, sexism, and corruption. The difference is that while *Carter Country* takes a more liberal (and condescending) stance toward most of its characters, the perspective of *The Dukes of Hazzard* is more squarely that of an inside (and self-serving) point of view, one suggestive of the shifting cultural tides at the turn of the decade.

Dukes wears its white southern working-class cultural values on its sleeve. The 1969 Dodge Charger Bo and Luke drive sports a Confederate flag painted on its roof and a car horn that plays "Dixie." That said, these racist gestures are not really central to a show whose primary purpose seems to serve as a vehicle for car chases. There is nevertheless a decidedly southern ideological ethos at work here. "This is Hazzard County. They do things different here," says Waylon Jennings in his voiceover in the opening episode. Jennings provided the theme song for the series and served as the narrator for its entire run; he appears as himself in the final season, as do the Oak Ridge Boys, Loretta Lynn, and Buck Owens at different points along the way. In the show's second episode, Jennings explains of the Dukes that "They fight the system. Any system." (With the apparent exception, one might add, of white supremacy.)

Such anti-establishmentarianism has long been a very real feature of white southern culture and politics, but of a decidedly different kind than that of the liberal counterculture that obscured it in the sixties and early seventies. Whereas the libertarianism of the New Left was focused on rejecting corporate and traditional sources of authority, the Right libertarianism of the South was defiant toward the moralistic reform projects of liberalism itself—essentially a protest against the protesters. This ingrained rebelliousness toward official authority of any kind dates at least as far back as Andrew Jackson. One can hear it, for example, in Lynyrd Skynyrd's 1974 hit "Sweet Home Alabama," with its praise for the segregationist George Wallace and its defiant question, "Watergate does not bother me / Does your conscience bother you?" To some extent, such white southerners regard the disdain with which they are regarded as a badge of pride. "If we weren't cousins, I'd marry you," Luke tells Daisy in that opening episode. "Never stopped anyone in this family before," she replies. Daisy herself is described by Jennings as a woman who "drives like Richard Perry, shoots like Annie Oakley, and knows all the words to Dolly Parton songs."

What's notable about *The Dukes of Hazzard*, though, is the way it takes this thoroughly grounded cultural milieu and positions it in a way that can ride a rising conservative tide. The voice for this project is Uncle Jessie, who lays it all out to his charges. "Makin' whiskey was a family tradition long before they [*sic*] was a U.S. of A. to tell us that we couldn't," he says early in the series. "And passin' the law didn't change the family ways." Later, around the dinner table, he tells his nephews, "For two hundred years, the Duke family had the whiskey craft. The government took that away from us. Then we had the land. And the Depression took that. Now all the Duke family has left is what it started with, and that's family." Free enterprise, the evils of regulation, family values: this was the Republican message in 1980.

Again, it is important to emphasize that *The Dukes of Hazzard* was not a political tract, such early exposition notwithstanding. Typical episodes involved the Dukes and their allies foiling any manner of Boss Hoggs's schemes (because they were on probation, the Duke brothers could not travel far and could not own guns, which is why they cultivated skills in shooting bows and arrows, another atavistic touch). But the show was very clearly a document of its time. It is also a show that is now taboo; in the aftermath of a South Carolina church shooting in 2015, the network TV Land pulled *Dukes* off its schedule, and Amazon.com stopped offering it through its free IMDb channel.[26] Yet the show continues to evoke fond memories across a wide spectrum of viewers.[27] How, and whether, it continues to be remembered remains to be seen.

J.R. survived. To be sure, his shooting was a setback, and it took him awhile to wrest back control of Ewing Oil from his brother Bobby. But audiences were counting on him to resume his wicked ways, and so he did for the rest of the decade, embodying a swashbuckling style of capitalism, which, alternatively thrilling and appalling, fascinated tens of millions of Americans each week in the age of Wall Street and Big Oil. *Dallas* plots—in more than one sense of that term—proliferated, cascaded, converged, and diverged. When the creators of the show and Patrick Duffy, who wanted out, concluded they had made a mistake by killing off Bobby Ewing at the end of the 1984–1985 season, they changed course in 1986–1987 by portraying his season-long death as a bad dream. By the time the series ended in 1991, it had become among the longest-running dramas in the history of television.

In an important sense, however, that run was just beginning. There were a total of five *Dallas* television movies between 1986 and 2007, and the series was rebooted in 2012 for a three-season run on the TNT network. Many of the original actors, including Hagman, returned for the revival, which focused on the power struggles between the adopted son of Pamela and Bobby and that of J.R. and Sue Ellen. Larry Hagman himself did not outlast his character, dying of throat cancer in 2012. The creators of the show concocted a complicated off-screen scheme in which we once again hear two gunshots, and once again engage in a new round of speculation about who did it. (The short answer is J.R. himself.)

But the significance of *Dallas* went beyond the durable appeal of the show itself. In its wake, a whole series of imitators followed. Technically, the first—*Knots Landing* (1979–1993)—was not derivative, since it had been conceived before *Dallas*. *Dynasty* (1981–1989) and *Falcon's Crest* (1981–1990) were also family dramas. But far more than *Dallas*, which for all its affluence could still evince an informal air (like characters in jeans), these series embraced the unapologetic opulence that burst into public view with Ronald Reagan's inaugural in 1981 and which remained a strand of eighties culture in the years that followed.

By this point, the socially minded dramas and sitcoms that had so dominated television at its literate peak in the early and mid-seventies had largely receded. Titillation was now less of a sexual nature (though that of course never disappeared) than material excess. Popular entertainment has always had a vicarious quality, and these were years in which conspicuous consumption was embraced as not-quite-guilty pleasures. In the words of Michael Douglas's Gordon Gekko of *Wall Street* (1987), "Greed is good." Gekko gets his comeuppance. But J.R.? That's not quite as clear.

In some cases, conservative ideology became more explicit on television in the eighties. The main character of *Too Close for Comfort* (1980–1987), who was played by *Mary Tyler Moore Show* veteran Ted Knight, was a right-wing cartoonist living in San Francisco. But perhaps the best example of the trend was the much-beloved sitcom *Family Ties* (1982–1990), in which Michael J. Fox played the conservative child of left-wing parents, which proved to be a fertile basis for comedy over many years. (His character's kid sister was politically apathetic—which in its own way was also a repudiation of the liberal reform project.)

But the rhythms of television have always been a little different, a little longer, than those of other popular media. When a book, movie, or song enters the national bloodstream, it is usually given a specific release date and enjoys a season of novelty when it is considered new. The lifespan of a TV show, however—especially a successful one—is measured in years, not seasons, of varying length. The old and new overlap each night on prime time (though successful shows in reruns become perennials in ways that resemble golden oldies radio stations or evergreen paperbacks). In that regard, TV time is a little more multidimensional. In their very porousness, TV shows resemble real life. How obvious; how strange.

CURRENCY

FIGURE 12. Milton Friedman in *Free to Choose*, the PBS series tied to his hugely bestselling 1980 book of the same name. Friedman became a key figure in neocon-servative economics for much the same reason that Ronald Reagan did in politics: an appealingly cheerful persona. And like Reagan, his influence would be durable. (Photofest)

CHAPTER 6

Turning the Page

The Publishing Industry in 1980

N JANUARY 1977, the British Broadcasting Corporation did a thoroughly unsurprising thing: it began running a documentary series on the history of economics, *The Age of Uncertainty*, featuring the well-known American economist John Kenneth Galbraith. (The series, which was also funded by the Canadian Broadcasting Company and a Los Angeles public television station, KCET, premiered on U.S. television later that year.) There are a number of reasons why this was unsurprising. The first is that the BBC had been enjoying a string of successful documentary series: *Civilization* (1969), hosted by art historian Sir Kenneth Clark; *America: A Personal History of the United States* (1972), starring journalist Alistair Cooke; and *The Ascent of Man*, a history of scientific thought by mathematician Jacob Bronowski (1973). All of these series spawned durably bestselling books. So it was only natural that BBC producer Adrian Malone, who had helped create *The Ascent of Man*—a play on Charles Darwin's famous 1871 book *The Descent of Man*—would develop a series on the social sciences. Like its predecessors, this one was to feature on-location backdrops in which scholars would inform and enlighten viewers with a deft touch. Moreover, Galbraith, a Harvard economist with a long track record of writing best-selling books, seemed like an obvious choice to host, not only as a popularizer (which made him suspect in the eyes of his more academic colleagues), but also as someone who appeared to embody the conventional wisdom of late twentieth-century economics: that which promoted a liberal industrial state run with a strong managerial, and redistributionist, hand.

By most reckonings, *The Age of Uncertainty* was a flop. Some of this was attributable to the production values of the series, which featured clumsy, even cheesy, reenactments of events and ideas. Some was a matter of Galbraith himself, a man who wrote with great facility but whose evident self-regard and formal manner on a TV screen were as likely to repel as disarm. And some was the implicitly unsatisfying premise of *The Age of Uncertainty,* a show that asserted the insufficiency of economics to explain reality, reflected in its title, which, as an otherwise approving reviewer in the *Washington Post* noted, was ironic coming from "a man who is rarely in doubt." More dismissive was the reaction of *New York Times* reviewer John J. O'Connor, who opened his assessment by saying "the science of economics remains surprisingly, if not distressingly, dismal."[1]

But the biggest challenge *The Age of Uncertainty* faced was ideological. Almost by definition, public television, insulated from the demands of the marketplace, has relied heavily on taxpayer funding, therefore giving its programming a leftward tilt. But by the late seventies, newly emboldened voices on the right called attention to the mandate of the Public Broadcasting Act of 1967, one that included "strict adherence to objectivity and balance in all programs or series of programs of a controversial nature." Galbraith himself was among those who replied to such criticism by noting that PBS fare included *Firing Line,* a talk show hosted by *National Review* founder William F. Buckley and *Wall $treet Week,* a weekly review on finance. But Arizona senator Barry Goldwater condemned *The Age of Uncertainty* as "socialistic propaganda," and the newly elected republican senator from Utah, Orrin Hatch, tried unsuccessfully to legislate balance into the network. In response to such concerns, PBS began including commentary at the end of each episode of *The Age of Uncertainty* that gave airtime to alternative views. So it was, for example, that California governor Ronald Reagan lamented Galbraith's apparent assumption that "leadership is best left to a group of wise mandarins on college campuses."

In a preemptive move, a libertarian think tank in London invited a rising star in economics, Milton Friedman, to give a lecture in response to *The Age of Uncertainty* before it even aired. Friedman, who won the 1976 Nobel Prize for economics, was a professor at the University of Chicago; he and Galbraith both owned homes in Vermont and referred to each other as friends. But there was little question that Friedman, who challenged the prevailing Keynesian orthodoxy that had held for nearly half a century, was now Galbraith's chief intellectual adversary.[2]

One person who sensed an opportunity here was Robert Chitester, manager of a small PBS station in Erie, Pennsylvania. A former liberal who had voted for George McGovern in 1972, Chitester had been converted to neoconservatism by Friedman's 1962 book *Freedom and Capitalism*, which he had read only months before Galbraith's series aired. Chitester had been introduced to Friedman by W. Allen Wallis, a free-market economist who had served as chancellor of the University of Rochester as well as chair of the Corporation for Public Broadcasting. Days after *The Age of Uncertainty* launched in England, Chitester contacted Friedman with a proposal: how about a conservative rejoinder to Galbraith?[3]

The timing was propitious. Friedman had used the proceeds from winning his Nobel Prize to buy an apartment in San Francisco, as he had recently been awarded an appointment at the Hoover Institution at Stanford University. Freed from the constraints of a regular professorship, he now considered following Galbraith's lead as a popularizer, though it took the prodding of his wife and collaborator, Rose, to nudge him toward acceptance. The basic idea was to promote the ideas in *Freedom and Capitalism*. The ten episodes that were planned would correspond to chapters in a new book, *Free to Choose*, that would be published to coincide with the series of the same name. It would air in January 1980.

In a portent of things to come, *Free to Choose* was developed in a significantly different way than *The Age of Uncertainty*. While the latter was financed solely from public TV stations that in turn had limited corporate support, the $2.8 million budgeted for *Free to Choose* was raised solely from outside sources well represented by Fortune 500 companies. As such, it pointed the way toward an evolving conversative media infrastructure that would prove to be powerful and influential in the decades that followed.

But *Free to Choose* differed not only in its origins or its argument but also in its mode of presentation—one which, by most reckonings, was significantly better than that of *The Age of Uncertainty*. Rather than rely on awkward dramatizations, each episode of *Free to Choose* was framed by a more journalistic—but also essayistic—analysis of key economic subjects like labor, consumers, education, and the like. Friedman's avowedly iconoclastic opinions were hedged by the series as "a personal statement." In fact, Galbraith had used the same phrase in his series, which he in turn had borrowed from Bronowski's *The Ascent of Man*. But to a much greater degree than either of these two cases, "a personal statement" effectively inoculated Friedman from charges that he was, as some nevertheless said of Galbraith, purveying false objectivity.

There were two other key factors that made *Free to Choose* different—and appealing. The first was the integration of a gallery of viewpoints into each episode. In contrast to the commentary appended to the American version of *The Age of Uncertainty*, each episode of *Free to Choose* included a freewheeling conversation among leading academic, corporate, and political figures who alternately contested or reinforced Friedman's point of view. This made for some truly compelling television that was notable for its intellectual diversity. So it was, for example, that one could see the conservative African American economist Thomas Sowell spar with the famed antipoverty scholar and activist Francis Fox Piven, or witness the intraracial black debate on the value of labor unions between the conservative Walter Williams and Jimmy Carter's assistant secretary of labor, Ernest Green.[4] The other X factor was Friedman himself, a man who lacked Galbraith's elegance, but nevertheless exuded an elfin charm that was hard to resist, even when you disagreed with him—a rhetorical asset

that Reagan, who *did* have a sense of elegance, perfected in the political arena.

The documentary version of *Free to Choose* became something of a
classic, a staple in the canon of right-wing media, where it remains
popular to this day. But it was ultimately the book version of *Free to
Choose*, adapted from series transcripts and cowritten with Rose
Friedman, that would really have legs. It spent six weeks atop the *New
York Times* bestseller list in the spring of 1980 and became the best-
selling nonfiction book of the year.[5] More importantly, *Free to Choose*
went on to become an iconic title of its era, and an evergreen paperback for half a century (the 1990 edition consulted for this chapter
was in its forty-third printing). While it would be an exaggeration to
call *Free to Choose* a latter-day *Wealth of Nations* or *Das Kapital*, Friedman nevertheless captured the spirit of his moment in a way that can
be usefully compared to Adam Smith or Karl Marx. Though his views
have long since gone out of vogue (even if, like Sigmund Freud, he
still has followers who tend to cherry-pick his ideas), *Free to Choose*
remains an important historical artifact.

The key to the book's success is that for all its evident erudition, the
prose is marked by great force and clarity. The Friedmans' message, in
brief, is the one Reagan would make the centerpiece of his presidency,
as expressed in his inaugural address: government as the problem,
not the solution. But the Friedmans were no slouches with epi-
grams, either. "A society that puts equality—in the sense of equality
of outcome—ahead of freedom will end up with neither equality or
freedom," they note at one point. (In the series, the line is delivered at
Thomas Jefferson's Monticello.) At another they say, "Voluntary
exchange is not a sufficient condition for prosperity and freedom. . . .
But voluntary exchange is a necessary condition for both prosperity
and freedom."[6]

The point here is less to affirm the Friedmans' views than their skill
in advancing them. This includes the shrewdness of the examples
they use to make their point. "Life is not fair," the couple notes in
their chapter on equality. "It is tempting to believe that government
can rectify what nature has spawned. But it is also important to

recognize how much we benefit from the very unfairness we deplore." They go on to note that "there's nothing fair about Marlene Dietrich's having been born with beautiful legs" before going on to a more contemporary example: "It is certainly not fair that Muhammad Ali should be able to earn millions of dollars in one night. But wouldn't it have been even more unfair to the people who enjoyed watching him if, in the pursuit of abstract ideal of equality, Muhammad Ali had not been permitted to earn more for one night's fight—or even each day preparing for a fight—than the lowest man on the totem pole could get for a day's unskilled work on the docks?" With reference to consumer protection, the Friedmans challenge the very premise of both government regulation and political activism: "Alternative sources of supply protect the consumer far more effectively than all the Ralph Naders of the world."[7]

Milton Friedman's ideas were met with strenuous objections, and, to his credit and that of other creators of the series, the disagreements are vividly registered in the documentary. By the early twenty-first century, much of the discourse had become outdated. State intervention in the economy has now been reaffirmed as a governing reality: the question is not *whether* the state should have a role in managing the economy, or in picking economic winners or losers, but rather if it can avoid doing so, whether it wants to or not. Actually, by the end of his life in 2006, Friedman himself had begun to hedge on a number of his ideas, among them a sunny optimism that capitalism would wear down Communist China, since a state-controlled private economy seemed like a contradiction in terms. "Bob," he told Chitester, "I ignored one fact. You have to have rule of law or my formula won't work."[8]

But more than anything else, the success of *Free to Choose* was less a matter of institutional support, a winning personality, or clear arguments than one of timing: a man had met his moment. "While Galbraith dwelled on the collapse of certainties in earlier eras, Friedman was busy propounding replacements to suit the needs of his own," notes economist Angus Burgin, whose 2013 article in the journal *History of Political Economy* chronicled this episode in the history of ideas.[9] Friedman was ahead of the curve in 1980, and he rode a rising tide to lead the intellectual vanguard for late twentieth-century neoliberalism. This made him not only lastingly influential, but a bona fide cultural phenomenon at the dawn of a new era. That status was ratified by his appearance on a TV show. But it was built on, and sustained by, that least sexy yet most durable of all the mass media: the book. Our lush pop culture landscape would be a desert without it.

The trade publishing business in 1980—which is to say a business based on reading as a form of entertainment, as opposed to educational textbooks or professional reference volumes—was what it always was: an industry in crisis. For as long as there have been people writing, editing, manufacturing, and distributing books, there have complaints about how hard, even impossible, its business model is: tiny advances, small print-runs, disappointing sales, mass indifference. For much of American history, books were relatively expensive luxury items, sometimes sold in local stores or via a subscription model, which is to say that books had to be bought before they could be printed—an approach that limited output. The birth of the Book-of-the-Month Club in 1926 offered a variation on the subscription model in which members would get curated titles delivered each month (the key is that they were sent without you asking for them), which raised the profiles of some writers. One important development in trade publishing was the appearance of paperback books in the 1930s, which not only offered readers a new level of affordability but also a huge amplification of access, as they could be sold in rack displays at retail outlets, such as drug stores. Paperbacks proliferated rapidly during and after the Second World War, aided by the explosion in college education, which prompted the rise of so-called trade paperbacks, larger and of higher quality than mass market paperbacks, in terms of both content and manufacturing. Most paperbacks at the time were reissued classics, or cheaper editions of hardcover books typically published a year or so earlier.

In the second half of the twentieth century, there was nostalgia in trade publishing in the first half the century, when the business was reputedly a gentlemanly profession of leisurely lunches and mutual lifetime commitments between writers and publishing houses (note the cozy domestic metaphor). Despite the relatively small scale, books as a medium—however small a fraction of revenue they generated compared with movies, television, and other media—were an indispensable source of content, providing the basis for countless films and shows, as well as radio and television programming. Such subsidiary rights were an important part of the publishing business in their commercial impact on the mass media as a whole, one reason why corporate conglomerates were always buying and selling publishing houses.

In our day, the snake in the book trade garden is the internet, which is a many-headed hydra, whether in the form of social media that eviscerate attention spans needed to read, or the Amazons who dominate the jungles of retailing. Before that, it was the megabooksellers like Barnes & Noble and Borders, which threatened to crush smaller independent stores in the 1990s before they themselves were besieged by Amazon. Their huge scale made appealing to customers seeking a wide selection, and publishers were glad to have a big outlet. But publishers of the nineties were also afraid of the leverage megachains could wield over them. Back in 1980, however, the threat was different: the small chain bookstore at the mall.

There were two in particular that dominated. The first was B. Dalton, which began as a spinoff of Dayton, a major retailer that sold books in its department stores (as indeed many department stores did). Named after family member Bruce Dalton, the company began as a bookstore chain in 1966 and spread rapidly from its base in the Midwest. Its principal challenger was Waldenbooks, a Connecticut-based company whose origins went back to the Great Depression, where it began as a book rental operation before transitioning to sales amid the paperback revolution.

By the seventies, Dalton and Walden were the Coke and Pepsi of book retailing. This was the golden age of the shopping mall, in which real estate companies curated shopping experiences for consumers by enticing a calibrated array of retailers—big anchor stores, specialty shops, fast food joints, handcart sellers—enclosed in large, climate-controlled spaces. Bookstores were an essential piece of this ecology, as reading was commonly regarded as a source of edification, entertainment, and spending, and as such was an attractive element in the retail mix. Mall culture was as much a science as it was an economic calculation, and bookstores were one more cog in a larger process of mass production.

Which, as far as publishers were concerned, was not necessarily a bad thing. The chains were reliable and efficient customers, in many ways ideal for houses looking for venues to move product. As befits the opportunistic nature of capitalism, chain stores also became literally contested spaces for publishers, as they sold prominent placement of particular titles for a price, making such marketing a standard part—which is to say cost—of the business.

The other key piece of this picture was scale. The chains were not only efficient; they also had the power to make or break a title on the basis of their orders. One of the lasting legacies of the Great Depression is that bookselling never ceased to be a consignment business: to entice retailers to take on stock, publishers promised them they could return what didn't sell. This could result in difficult decisions about print runs (too few and you'll have disappointed customers; too many and you'll be drowning in expensive inventory). The imperative, then, was to sell as many books as possible—and to concentrate on potential hits that would sell massively and quickly. So it was that the book business, on a smaller scale, followed bigger cultural industries like movies and music toward a blockbuster model.

The most obvious manifestation of scale was the concept of "wallpapering"—large displays of a single title at the front of bookstores to convey a sense of mass popularity, with the idea of communicating that the title in question was the new hot thing, a conversation you would be eager to join. Such tactics spoke to the growing commodification of book culture. In fact, the books that were going to be bestsellers could be known months in advance based on the size of the advances authors received, their print runs, the sale of subsidiary rights, and the advertising resources that were devoted to them.

Which is not to say that there were no flops (one aspect of the market was the practice of remaindering, or selling books at a fraction of their original price as a way of clearing warehouse space). But the business was routinized to an unprecedented degree by this time, reflecting the extent to which publishing houses, typically divisions within larger media conglomerates, had been integrated into the fabric of late twentieth-century consumer capitalism.

The crucial incentive in this approach to publishing was discounting: slashing prices for big-name hardcover books so that consumers would regard them as bargains worth buying sooner rather than waiting for a paperback edition to appear. One publishing figure who was particularly notable in making the most of this tactic was Leonard Reggio of Barnes & Noble. The company, a chain whose roots date back to the nineteenth century, had dwindled to a single store in downtown Manhattan in 1971, when Reggio bought it and went all in on discounting, which turned the company into a publishing colossus (and one that would virtually swallow the college textbook business along the way). But the mall retailers were also at the forefront of this trend, one in which sellers would price titles anywhere from 10 to 35 percent off what was listed on the inside flap of the front cover. Retailers typically paid 60 percent of the price of every book sold, which made their margins small, but they made up for it in volume. One way to sustain such momentum involved creating literary franchises, whether in characters (like Spenser, the fictive detective in Robert B. Parker's series) or authors (like Mary Higgins Clark) who reliably delivered books each year to be published, retailed, and sold on an industry conveyor belt. The literary franchise predates this period—Ian Fleming's James Bond and Mickey Spillane's Mike Hammer novels were fixtures of the fifties and sixties—but they became refined and routinized via chain discounting by 1980. This model, in one form or another, has been with us ever since, though nowadays, it's big box retailers like Costco and Target who practice it on the largest scale.

As with other industries, there have always been multiple ways to measure a book's popularity, both with the public and within a given media industry. In pop music, for example, the mainstay has long been *Billboard* magazine. In terms of book publishing sales and prestige, it is the *New York Times* Bestseller List, printed Sunday in the *New York Times Book Review*, which has been a weekly feature of the newspaper since 1896. The NYTBR list has always been notorious for its lack of transparency, and for possible distortions like mass-buying of titles by interest groups to influence placement on the list. But it nevertheless remains a reasonably good way to provide a snapshot of publishing in 1980, with a particular focus on those books, fiction and nonfiction, that managed to occupy the top slot that year.

When viewed in this light, the success of *Free to Choose* becomes a vivid case study of the ways ideas get popularized and pumped into the culture at large, a process amplified by book reviews, author interviews, and other elements of a publishing publicity apparatus that was fully in place in 1980. To be sure, Milton and Rose Friedman were not quite in the same league as brand-name authors of suspense novels or celebrity memoirs (the biggest of these in 1980 were those of the rising talk show host Phil Donahue and the two-time Oscar winner Shelley Winters, whose *Shirley: Also Known as Shelley* topped the *Times* nonfiction list as a summer beach read in 1980). But a quick look at the industry helps explain how it is that new ideas moved into society and were absorbed in the culture at large. This, in short, is the way change happens, though it is not always a quick process.

In surveying the biggest books of 1980 in retrospect, it is hard to avoid concluding that when it comes to reading fare, American literary culture was still firmly anchored in the seventies. Perhaps this reflects the fact that books are typically created over a period of years, compared with a movie, which, however tortured its production process, is usually completed in months, or a pop record, whose gestation may be measured in weeks. Whatever the explanation, it does appear that on the whole, the bestselling books of 1980 tended to look more backward to preoccupations characteristic of the early to mid-seventies rather than the emerging neocon dispensation. They seem less responsive to changing cultural currents than hits in other media.

This was certainly true of the book atop the *Times* bestseller list in the first two weeks of 1980: Kurt Vonnegut's *Jailbird*. Vonnegut, who began his writing career in the fifties known for the science fiction genre, achieved mainstream literary success in 1969 with *Slaughterhouse Five*, a fierce antiwar novel that reflected his experiences as an infantryman in the Second World War as well as an infusion of absurdism that would be a lingering motif in his body of work. Like *M*A*S*H*, a TV show about the Korean War that functioned as an allegory of the Vietnam War, *Slaughterhouse Five* was similarly embraced as a document of the countercultural left at a time when antiwar sentiment was at its height—and hostility toward Richard Nixon, who prosecuted it, was also at fever pitch.

Befitting such origins, *Jailbird* is a Watergate novel. It opens with the hapless protagonist, Walter F. Starbuck, finishing a jail sentence because he unwittingly allowed a trunk full of illegal campaign contributions to be stored in his White House office (and that office happened to be directly below where the Watergate conspiracy was hatched). Starbuck had worked as President Nixon's adviser on youth affairs; he got the job because a decade and a half earlier, he had unwittingly destroyed the career of a college classmate by mentioning his communist background amid the McCarthyite witch hunts that had brought Nixon to national prominence. But Nixon seemed to regard Starbuck more with contempt than gratitude, as suggested by the virtually meaningless, if not ironic, position Starbuck gave him, since Nixon's relationship with American youth at the time was widely regarded as a nonstarter. Starbuck seems to take the appointment without pride or ambition, since he doesn't seem to have a higher opinion of himself than anyone else does.

But Vonnegut's own ambitions for *Jailbird* seem considerably higher than rendering a Watergate satire. The story spans much of the twentieth century, including the labor struggles of factory workers, the notorious Sacco and Vanzetti case in which two Italian anarchists were wrongly put to death, and a critique of conglomerate capitalism in the form of the rapacious RAMJAC corporation. Vonnegut's alter ego, Kilgore Trout, makes an appearance here, as he does in a number of Vonnegut novels. But the moral of the story seems simple, if not trite: a secular affirmation of the Sermon on the Mount in which the meek are the blessed ones. Vonnegut was clearly a chronicler of his times, at times an amusing one. But in this book, he seems as melancholy and lost as his protagonist, capable of little more than skeptical riffing in a climate of cultural exhaustion.

A similar sense of melancholy, albeit a more tough-minded one, emerges in the novel that displaced *Jailbird* from the top slot: John le Carré's *Smiley's People*. Like Vonnegut, le Carré, a former agent in Britain's MI6 intelligence service, was a veteran novelist—and a novelist veteran—anchored in genre fiction, in his case spy novels. He first came into international prominence with his 1963 thriller *The Spy Who Came in from the Cold*. Unlike Vonnegut, however, le Carré remained committed to the thriller even as he gained plaudits reserved for the most ambitious writers of literary fiction. *Smiley's People* was the third installment of le Carré's so-called Karla series (after *Tinker Tailor Soldier Spy* in 1974 and *The Honourable Schoolboy* in 1977), in which his protagonist George Smiley matches wits with his Soviet antagonist, Karla. There's never any question in le Carré's work about the evil of the Soviet system, even as the author recognizes shades of complexity in his Eastern bloc characters and the moral ambiguities inherent in Western intelligence—and Western society as a whole (he's no fan of the United States). As such, le Carré's novels reflected the larger imaginative landscape of détente, even as the New Right was beginning to articulate an intellectual blueprint for finally winning the Cold War. *Smiley's People* was made into a BBC miniseries in 1982; Smiley would make a valedictory appearance in le Carré's final novel, *A Legacy of Spies* (2017).

One spy novelist with a lot less ambivalence than le Carré who also made an appearance on the bestseller lists in 1980—though never quite attaining the top slot—was William F. Buckley, the well-known conservative raconteur and founder of the *National Review* who dabbled in fiction on the side. Buckley's 1980 novel *Who's on First*, the third in his series featuring CIA protagonist Bradford Oakes, depicts "Blackie" matching wits with his Soviet adversaries amid the space race and the Soviet invasion of Hungary in 1956. While Buckley's bona fides as a conservative were beyond dispute, he represented a more avowedly elitist version than the emergent populist varieties propounded by figures such as Friedman and Reagan, even if their critics nevertheless considered them alike in their hostility toward welfare-state egalitarianism.

Another spy writer whose work really did point, however haltingly, toward a post–Cold War geopolitics was Robert Ludlum, whose 1980 novel *The Bourne Identity* spent sixteen weeks at number one in the spring and summer, the longest stretch of any book that year. The first installment of a trilogy whose literary and cinematic legs carried the franchise well into the twenty-first century, the novel involves the career of a U.S. government operative whose head injury off the coast of France results in amnesia that leads him to spend the rest of the novel recovering his personal history. As the man known to himself and others as Jason Bourne learns, he was a Special Forces agent in Vietnam who became an assassin for the CIA, which now considers him a renegade. Meanwhile, Bourne also contends with the enemy known as Carlos, a Venezuelan-born, Soviet-trained mercenary. Like le Carré, Ludlum depicts Americans as amoral at best in protecting their interests. But in establishing a main plotline in which Bourne's nemesis does not fit neatly into a Cold War paradigm—Carlos has an agenda that extends far beyond that of his Soviet mentors—Ludlum focuses his gaze on new global conflicts that increasingly defined the American imperial imagination.

Another popular novelist in 1980 with a similar skepticism toward secret U.S. government behavior was Stephen King, whose novel *Firestarter* topped the bestseller list in early fall that year. As was his wont, King set his books slightly in the future from when he wrote them—this one actually reaches its climax in October 1980, just as the book reached its commercial peak on bookstore shelves. King's fiction often features seemingly ordinary people who find themselves confronting supernatural forces, whether internal or external. In this case the one in question is pyrokinesis, which belongs to a five-year-old girl named Charlie McGee, who causes spontaneous combustion when emotionally agitated, apparently as a result of her father Andy and mother Vicky participating in medical experiments secretly supervised by the CIA (or "the Shop," as it is referred to in the book) while they were college students. Vicky, who developed telekinetic powers, is later murdered for refusing to reveal the whereabouts of her daughter, and Andy, who has fled with Charlie, has the power to control other people's behavior, though the effort is deeply enervating for him. Charlie, by contrast, is a human dynamo, and The Shop kidnaps father and daughter so as to harness her powers for geopolitical ends. It should surprise no one that Andy's Everyman will eventually outwit the evil government bureaucrats, in part with the help of other Good Americans. In an afterword to *Firestarter*, King explains that the U.S. government has, in fact, administered dangerous drugs to unwitting subjects, and that while his tale is unquestionably fictive, he did mean to suggest that "the world, although well-lighted with fluorescents and incandescent bulbs and neon, is still full of unsettling nooks and crannies"[10]—a statement that in many ways sums up his larger career project. *Firestarter* became a 1984 movie starring Drew Barrymore as Charlie, in a cast that included Heather Locklear, Martin Sheen, and George C. Scott. King's novel *The Dead Zone*, about a man who awakens from a coma to find himself clairvoyant, was a *Times* bestseller in 1979, and lasted on the list into 1980.

All of the books here were written by—and, probably more often than not, for—men. As in other industries, men dominated publishing, where on any given week a dozen or more of the top fifteen novels were written by them. There were nevertheless women novelists with commercial appeal and influence, like Marilyn French—her 1977 novel *The Women's Room* sold 20 million copies and became notorious for its famous line "all men are rapists, that's all they are"—who appeared on the 1980 list with *The Bleeding Heart*, a novel about a divorcée and a married man who have a torrid affair after meeting on a train.[11] Such transgressive scenarios were indicative of the way women were seeking wider and more complex experiences in popular fiction.

By far the bestselling novel by a woman in 1980 was *Princess Daisy*, by Judith Krantz, which spent five weeks in the top slot in February and March. (Paperback rights for the book sold for $3.2 million months before it was released.)[12] Krantz, a magazine writer and fashion editor who turned to fiction late in life, first scored success with her 1978 novel *Scruples,* a novel about an overweight goose who becomes a svelte swan and founds the boutique of the title. In a similar vein, *Princess Daisy* is a fairy tale—of a very historically specific kind. Marguerite Alexandrovna Valensky (aka Daisy) is indeed a princess, daughter of a prerevolutionary Russian aristocrat and an American movie star. Her difficult childhood includes the death of her parents, a mentally disabled twin sister to whom she is deeply attached, and a brutish half-brother who sexually assaults her. Daisy nevertheless overcomes adversity by attending the University of California at Santa Cruz, entering the advertising business, and, of course, finding the man of her dreams.

But since the heart of the story took place in the 1970s, the retrograde elements of *Princess Daisy* had to be adapted (or camouflaged) for a feminist age. One thing this means is that the novel is sexually frank to the point of pornography, yet rendered in prose laden with lingering Victorian accents. "When he mounted her and she opened for him, a queen joyfully squandering her treasures, it was a primeval act," Krantz writes of the congress of Daisy's parents. A socially prominent gay man and lesbian woman enjoy a marriage of convenience that leads to a series of trysts that litter the book. "In their own inner circle, they were not only recognized as brilliantly successful deceivers," the narrator explains of closeted life, "but applauded for their cleverness in finding each other and using each other so well. They had understood the secret, so rarely brought out in its raw and naked state; the fact that among the successful of the world, there is *no gender*—there is only success or lack of success."[13]

It is also important that Cinderella have a career. Daisy becomes an important account executive, albeit one who has to endure her fair share of sexism. "'That boy will go far. I like his fucking nerve,'" her boss says approvingly of a colleague. "Sure you do, Daisy thought balefully, in a man. But let a woman try it and you wouldn't merely threaten to tear her head off, you'd cut her heart out and eat it for breakfast." At another point in the story, her future husband, a self-made corporate executive, asserts that "faded gentility and purity are *out*! We are going to capture today's most lucrative market: the working woman—dynamic, adventurous, and *with her own paycheck*." He insists that the face of the new cosmetic campaign in question should be Daisy herself. He will later dub her "an American working girl who also happens to be a princess."[14] *Princess Daisy* suggests both the impact feminism was making in popular consciousness as the seventies gave way to the eighties, but also its limits on the cusp of an era where large numbers of women would find themselves proverbially saying "I'm not a feminist, but. . . ."

It wasn't only women who were grappling with these issues. *Princess Daisy* was knocked from the top slot by *The Bourne Identity*, but Ludlum's book was in turn displaced by Sidney Sheldon's *Rage of Angels*, which spent eleven weeks at number one between July and September 1980. Sheldon was a true renaissance man in the entertainment industry—and one who specialized in writing about women. Dubbed "the elder statesman of commercial fiction," Sheldon actually began his career in Hollywood, where he won an Oscar for his screenplay for the 1947 film *The Bachelor and the Bobby-Soxer*. He moved on to Broadway, where he netted a Tony award in 1959 for *Redhead*, a musical. Sheldon then entered television, where he created and wrote for several shows, notably *I Dream of Jeannie* (1965–1970), for which he received an Emmy award nomination. At age fifty, he turned his hand to fiction; Sheldon's first novel, *The Other Side of Midnight* (1978), was an immediate smash. As of this writing, there are 300 million of his books in print. Many of his readers were—and are—women. "I like to write about women who are talented and capable, but most important, retain their femininity," he once said. "Women have tremendous power—their femininity, because men can't do without it."[15]

But Sheldon, no less than Krantz, had to also furnish those readers with credible professional aspirations for those women characters. In the case of *Rage of Angels*, his protagonist is Jennifer Parker, a young lawyer who finds herself caught between a crusading district attorney and an alluring gangster. She manages to retain her independence and achieve a notable degree of success as an attorney. Sheldon structures the book with a series of subplots redolent of a television series: Parker wins an acquittal for a black man facing a death sentence, gains a paternity settlement for a woman with a baby, collects damages for another woman hit by a truck, and frees a woman confined to a nursing home by her greedy relatives. But she pays a heavy price in a climax that results in the loss of much of what she holds dear, and in this regard, it is possible to discern a suggestion, witting or not, that gender emancipation may not be worth the cost. Whether or not such messages were productive, it is clear that millions of women were buying them, literally and figuratively, in a time of widespread gender ambivalence.

The pull of the past was evident in other ways too. The top slot on the *Times* fiction bestseller list for the final months of 1980 was occupied by historical novels. The first of these was Ken Follett's *The Key to Rebecca*, a title that pays homage to the classic 1938 Daphne Du Maurier novel, which figures prominently in the plot. Welshman Follett, a former journalist specializing in spy thrillers, enjoyed international success with *The Eye of the Needle* (1978) and *Triple* (1979) before scoring again with this one, a story based in fact and set during the German campaign against Britain in North Africa during World War II. The imperial backdrop of the story appeared neither troubling to Follett nor, it would seem, to his audience. "Yes. We're not very admirable, especially in our colonies, but the Nazis are worse, whether the Egyptians know it or not," his protagonist, William Vandam, observes at one point. "In England, decency is making slow progress; in Germany it's taking a big step backward."[16] By the time Follett's book was published in 1980, the Second World War had been over for 35 years—a long time, but well within the living memory of many of his readers, who no doubt experienced the novel as comfort food. One suspects that similar forces were at work in the novel that closed out the year on the *Times* list, James Michener's *The Covenant*. Michener, who specialized in multigenerational sagas, focuses in this one on the evolution of modern South Africa from prehistoric times until the 1970s in a book stuffed with historical exposition.

This was, notably, about as close to any kind of black life that appeared on the *Times* bestseller list in 1980. No African Americans landed on it—a remarkable testimony of racial exclusion in the nation's popular literary culture, and something that is notable given the black presence in other media, whether robust in the case of popular music, or less so, but still evident, in the case of television. Clearly, there were limits in the American fictive imagination, though Toni Cade Bambara's experimental novel *The Salt Eaters* was published by Random House that year, to be followed months later by Toni Morrison's *Tar Baby* in the spring of 1981. The coming years would also bring Alice Walker's *The Color Purple* and Gloria Naylor's *The Women of Brewster Place* (both 1982), indicative of a coming wave that would only build in ensuing years and decades. But in publishing terms, 1980 was a racial desert.

If bestselling American fiction was still stuck somewhere in the seventies in 1980, bestselling nonfiction was inhabiting the sixties—more specifically, the sex revolution of the sixties, which continued to preoccupy readers and writers long afterward. Two of the seven books that occupied the top slot on the *Times* nonfiction bestseller list focused on its enduring legacy.

The first of these, Nancy Friday's *Men in Love*, reached the summit on May 18. Friday, a pop sociologist, first came to national attention in 1973 with her book *My Secret Garden: Women's Sexual Fantasies*. The book is what might be termed an erotic ethnography in that it collects first-person accounts, organized by themes. As such, *My Secret Garden* wandered into fraught terrain, not so much from guardians of Victorian morality than feminists whose relationship with sexuality was often ambivalent. "This woman is not a feminist," *Ms.* magazine asserted at the time, prompting Friday to respond, "Sexual freedom was never part of modern feminism, never celebrated as such at Feminism Headquarters." Friday followed up *The Secret Garden* with a sequel, *Forbidden Flowers* (1975), before going on to write her best-known book, *My Mother, My Self: The Daughter's Search for Identity* (1977), which shifted her gaze to this key parent–child relationship. *Men in Love*, which followed three years later, in effect turned the tables, rendering male versions of fantasies in a similar manner to that of *My Secret Garden*. As Friday told *People* magazine, "The major theme in men's sexual fantasies is the sexually aroused woman. It's still hard for most men to believe that women enjoy sex," a comment indicative of the way midcentury attitudes about sexuality persisted.[17]

Men in Love was succeeded on the best-seller list one week later by another book that spent ten weeks at the top, and considered an innovation as much in form as it was in content: Gay Talese's *Thy Neighbor's Wife*. The book is a complex and sprawling piece of journalism, one that ranges from a sketch of the nineteenth-century anti-smut reformer Anthony Comstock to an extended profile of Hugh Hefner and the rise of *Playboy*, whose commercial fortunes are at the beginning of a slow decline as the book ends.[18] The heart of *Thy Neighbor's Wife*, though, is a set of ethnographically minded portraits of (generally) ordinary Americans and their encounter with the sexual revolution of the 1960s and 1970s. This approach goes to the core of Talese's argument—which is that what made the revolution revolutionary is how deeply it suffused American society. "While the blasphemous, bra-less, peace-bearded young counterculturalists received most of the attention in the media during the sixties, multitudes of middle-class married people were also involved in this quest for free expression and more control over their bodies," he notes. This could be unsettling, he shows, but also exhilarating, especially for women. As one husband ruefully realizes, "He had enjoyed the bodies of many women and had become unhappy only after [his wife] Judith had begun to assert her own independence."[19] In a twist that generated some controversy, Talese ends the book with a final chapter in which he is a participant-observer, reporting—in the third person—on his sexual experiences at a massage parlor and a nudist colony. He describes the strains it put on his marriage (to Nan Talese, a major figure in the New York publishing industry). It survived.

Talese also reports developments that suggest the shifting tides in American sexuality at century's end. His account of the 1973 Supreme

Court obscenity case *Miller v. California,* in which the court decided that obscene materials do not enjoy First Amendment protection, describes Chief Justice Warren Burger's articulation of "community standards" as a matter of pushing power away from the federal government toward local communities in a manner consonant with the libertarianism that would dominate conservative politics in the coming decade. The implications of that ruling assumed sharper outlines in *Hamling v. United States* (1974), which Talese reports scrupulously, though with implicit sympathy toward the defendants who were convicted of sending pornographic material by mail. Despite the fact that the locus of *Thy Neighbor's Wife* is clearly the years before these cases, Talese does seem to sense which way the more conservative ideological winds were blowing as his narrative ends.

Some of those winds blew down prospects for Talese's story to spread more widely. As he relates in an afterword to the 2009 edition of the book, film rights for *Thy Neighbor's Wife* were sold to United Artists for $2.5 million. Pulitzer prize–winning playwright Marsha Norman was hired to write the script, and William Friedkin was slated to direct. But the *Heaven's Gate* fiasco dragged down the project, and while the book continued to sell well, the rise of AIDS and wide reporting on the spread of genital herpes generated new skepticism about the efficacy of the permissive sexual culture that the book described. *Thy Neighbor's Wife* morphed from a cutting-edge account of a new cultural phenomenon into a piece of social history valued today as a primary source document of the past.[20]

Another nonfiction bestseller in 1980 became dated even more quickly—and badly. Douglas Casey's *Crisis Investing: Opportunities and Profits in the Coming Great Depression* appeared when the nation was deep in the throes of economic malaise. While it is true that the U.S. economy fell into a severe recession in the early eighties—which we tend to forget amid the euphoria and nostalgia of the later boom that was to some degree a matter of expertly managed public relations by the Reagan White House—the Great Depression of Casey's title never materialized. A self-described "anarcho-capitalist" and classmate of future president Bill Clinton, Casey struck publishing gold because he was able to tap the established genre of finance books, a genre that coexisted alongside diet books, self-help, and humor.[21] Such books inhabited the best-seller lists in 1980, and continue to do so to this day.

However, the title that spent the final eight weeks of the year atop the nonfiction *Times* bestseller list—Carl Sagan's *Cosmos*—was important because it marked the arrival of a new genre of bestseller: the pop science book. Sagan, an astronomer, had a career that compares instructively with that of Galbraith and Friedman. Like them, he began in academe after attending the University of Chicago while Friedman was there (and like Friedman, he was of Ukrainian descent). Like Galbraith, Sagan was regarded as a little too accessible for his own good, and was denied tenure at Harvard (he landed at Cornell). Like both of them, he starred in a PBS series that he cowrote. *Cosmos*, a survey of the universe, first aired on the network in the fall of 1980 and was an instant success, ultimately seen by hundreds of millions of people in dozens of countries around the world. It was the most-watched documentary in TV history until Ken Burns's *The Civil War* came along a decade later. The accompanying book, issued in different formats over ensuing years, has also sold millions of copies.[22]

One reason for Sagan's success is that he captured Friedman's sunny disposition without the polemical baggage. He wrote and spoke with comparable clarity, as fascinated by the extrapolations of the ancients in understanding the universe as he was with modern science. Sagan's range and accessibility opened up a new vista in popular culture that would later be filled by figures ranging from Bill Bryson to Neil deGrasse Tyson. "He stepped in places where no one stepped before," Tyson, who achieved similar stature as an astronomer, later noted. "He was criticized for appearing, for example, on Johnny Carson's show. That's entertainment! That's not science! Then people realized, Oh, my gosh, the public embraces what we do as scientists. Now no one would object to such a thing."[23]

Like *Free to Choose*, the success of *Cosmos* is again a reminder of how deeply entwined trade publishing was with other media in 1980. Books furnished the basis of content on other platforms, and those platforms in turn became a springboard for commercial success measured in sales and visibility at the local mall. In the twenty-first century, such synergy has become so important that it would be virtually impossible for an author to land on the bestseller list, or even get published, without it. Bigger was not only better; better *meant* bigger. Becoming a writer didn't disappear as an aspiration. But despite that fact, there were more avenues than ever to pursue it, even as the likelihood of success steadily receded from view.

There is another number one bestseller of the time worth discussing here, albeit one that doesn't fit into traditional publishing categories. Like the works that have been the focus of this study, it managed to look backward and forward at the same time, offering a vivid snapshot of a culture in transition.

Like the canniest observers of American culture, Lisa Birnbach was an outsider who got in while managing to maintain a degree of cheeky detachment. The daughter of Jewish immigrants, she grew up on the Upper East Side of Manhattan and attended Riverdale Country Day, an elite prep school in the leafy Riverdale section of the Bronx. She received her bachelor's degree from Brown in the new field of semiotics in 1978 and got a job working at hipster heaven: *The Village Voice,* where she cowrote its "Scenes" column. She and her editor had an idea for a novelty book on lightbulb jokes that they took to Workman Publishing, which specialized in the genre. The reaction they got was tepid, but Birnbach was buttonholed at the company's office by another Workman employee who had heard of her from a mutual acquaintance. This person had assembled a team of copywriters, photographers, and illustrators for a project she was supervising, and wondered if Birnbach would be interested in editing the text. Birnbach took the job, and about three months later *The Official Preppy Handbook* was published. ("Look Muffy, a book for us," reads the tagline on the cover.) It was an instant hit, going to the top of the *Times* trade paperback list—original, as opposed to reprint, paperback editions of editorial content were still a new idea at the time— and remained there for months. Part of the reason, she speculated, is

PREP QUEEN

FIGURE 13. Grace Kelly in a publicity still from 1954. A product of Philadelphia's Main Line, Kelly embodied the apotheosis of a prep culture that moved from margins to center with the publication of Lisa Birnbach's novelty bestseller *The Preppie Handbook* in 1980. Kelly, who would become Princess Grace upon her marriage to Prince Rainer of Monaco in 1956, was widely mourned after her death in a car crash in 1982. (Photofest)

that *The Official Preppy Handbook* landed between the cracks in the intensifying struggle for space in bookstores. It was small, relatively inexpensive, and often placed near the cash register, allowing it to pick up momentum as an impulse buy. By the end of 1980 over 400,000 copies were in circulation. The book remains in print to this day.[24]

No one was more surprised by its success than Birnbach herself, whose nickname was Bunny. "I did not think this book would have any interest or appeal to anyone who was not already familiar with it," she remembered forty years later. As Birnbach noted, *The Official Preppy Handbook* was conceived and produced during what were still the Carter years. "In New York, we didn't know that old money was going to matter." Birnbach added that "most of the preppies I knew in college were Democrats," pointing to the legacies of John F. Kennedy and Franklin Delano Roosevelt, both of whom had prep credentials (the latter far more than the former, who in another day would have been disqualified by his Irish Catholicism). In publicizing the project then and since, Birnbach claimed that prep was less an economic state than a state of mind. "Preppies are the original inflation fighters," she said in 1981 of the preppy emphasis on durable goods. But as Birnbach at least implicitly recognized, this was disingenuous, as she conveyed with a wink. "It is the inalienable right of every man, woman, and child to wear khaki," the book's opening reads. "Looking, acting, and ultimately being a prep is not restricted to an elite minority lucky enough to attend prestigious private schools, just because an ancestor or two happened to arrive on the *Mayflower*. You don't even have to be a registered Republican. In a true democracy everyone can be upper class and live in Connecticut. It's only fair."[25]

The Official Preppy Handbook, stuffed with sidebars, drawings, and charts, is organized into seven chapters tracing the life cycle of a prep from birth to retirement. A major reason why the book works as well as it does is its intimacy with the world it describes, rendered in a key of light irony. "Daddy often proclaims he got where he is through hard work, sacrifice, and denial of immediate pleasure for future good and that grandfather's trust fund is no reason to slack off," a chapter on the preppy value system notes. A chapter on old money explains that "the thing about money is that it's nice that you have it. You're not excited to get it. You don't talk about it. It's like a golden retriever by a chair—when you reach out for it, it's there."[26]

At the same time, the underlying assumption of the book is that for all their affluence, the White Anglo-Saxon Protestant foundations of American society are no longer dominant, because WASPs are a desiccated elite who have become more charming than oppressive. The governing logic of their schooling, the handbook explains, is Horatio Alger in reverse: "No one is more boring than the person who comes to prep school to *study*." A sidebar on the Ivy League notes that while it was once Preppy heaven, the impact of meritocracy was already being felt: "Students are accepted largely for academic achievement, rather on the basis of whether they will fit in with a campus 'mood.'" (Such terminology of "fit" was once the basis upon which Jews like Birnbach, and, later, Asian-Americans, were denied admission to places like Brown and the lingering preppy haven of Princeton.) A chapter on school athletics notes, "One of the most endearing things about a Preppy is his ability to say 'nicely played' when he has just sprawled on his face and narrowly missed a shot, and to sincerely congratulate the winner of a game he has just lost. (Sportsmanship is also the reason why, despite their competitive training, Preppies do not actually run the world.)" When, in a chapter on midlife, the manual notes that "what Preppies don't need are good public schools and a shopping mall," the line is at once a comment on their snobbery but also their irrelevance from the mainstream of American life.[27]

The clever acuity of such observations notwithstanding, this underlying premise is not quite true. Yes, Ronald Reagan—the son of an alcoholic shoe salesman from small-town Illinois who made his career in Hollywood—was the Republican nominee for president in 1980. But his running mate, George Herbert Walker Bush, was the son of a U.S. senator from Connecticut, and Bush himself attended Greenwich Country Day School, Philips Andover Academy, and Yale before heading to Texas and becoming a (not entirely convincing) oil man and then returning to his blueblood roots in the diplomatic corps as U.S. ambassador to China and head of the Central Intelligence Agency. Prepsters were no longer dominant, but they hardly disappeared.

And yet it was the perception that prep culture was now a *sub*culture that allowed it to emerge as a cultural trend in the years following publication of *The Official Preppy Handbook*. Prepdom had an air of retrograde novelty. This is not something Birnbach and her collaborators pulled off single-handedly—one can discern it, for example, in the sentimentally scatological frat-house comedy *Animal House* in 1978—or, one should technically say, *National Lampoon's Animal House*, as the movie grew out of *National Lampoon*, a magazine run out of (preppy) Harvard. But *The Official Preppy Handbook* rode an emerging wave of nostalgia for the glory days of the American empire in ways that *could* be appropriated as fad because the impulse was more symbolic than rooted in material conditions. In years to come, the trappings of prep could be seen everywhere, from fashion, to pop music, and yes, in the cultural—and economic—revival of the Ivy League, which had become a bit scruffy by the seventies. Like all fads, it was noted, resisted, and ultimately faded *as* a fad. Other aspects would prove more durable.

The future had arrived. It looked like yesterday. You could read all about it. At the mall.

FIGURE 14. President Jimmy Carter announcing sanctions actions against Iran, April 7, 1980. Public opinion rallied around Carter at the outset of the crisis, but growing doubts about his leadership would dog his campaign, his increasingly grim persona at odds with the toothy smile he rode to victory in 1976. (Marion S. Trikosko, Library of Congress / Wikimedia Commons)

CHAPTER 7

Inflection Point

Autumn 1980

I
T IS LATE AUGUST 1980. One hit sequel movie, *Smokey and the Bandit II*, has displaced another, *The Empire Strikes Back*, for the top slot at the box office. Aussie Olivia Newton-John is riding high on the pop charts with "Magic." *Dallas* and *The Dukes of Hazzard* are finishing a cycle of summer repeats on the eve of a new television season. Sidney Sheldon's *Rage of Angels* is right smack in the middle of its run as the beach read of the year. Escapism is the order of the day; a new school year looms.

The waning weeks of summer are customarily considered the quietest stretch in a presidential election year, and 1980 was no exception. The campaign began in earnest with the bustle of primary season in January, enthusiasm for which had been building for months, as it always does. Ronald Reagan had largely captured the Republican nomination by spring. Facing a primary challenge from Ted Kennedy, Jimmy Carter's fight for renomination by the Democrats wasn't fully over until summer. The GOP held its convention in mid-July; the Democrats followed in mid-August. General election campaigns unofficially kick off after Labor Day, by which point summer vacations are usually over, and the electorate at large—specifically that segment of which may not have been paying attention but will start to—becomes the central preoccupation of campaigns now vying to appeal beyond their party lines in the general election. But in late

August, that moment had not quite arrived, and for many voters (or, more to the point, nonvoters), there wasn't much to look forward to, or choose from, in the lackluster set of candidates: an uninspiring incumbent, an "amiable dunce,"[1] and an irrelevant third-party candidacy of John Anderson, who was not gaining any traction.

Of course, there's no off-season for politicos and poll watchers, and there were any number of fingers in the wind that August. The indications at that point seemed to be tilting toward Carter. As was generally true of most nominees of the time, he came out of the Democratic National Convention with a bump in a Gallup poll in late August, picking up seven points while Reagan lost six, giving Reagan a one-point lead.[2]

In the eyes of mainstream media watchers, Reagan wasn't doing himself any favors. In a speech for the Veterans of Foreign Wars in Chicago on August 18—the group broke with eighty years of neutrality to endorse him—Reagan described the Vietnam War as "a noble cause," provoking outrage. *Washington Post* columnist Joseph Kraft called the remark divisive; the more horse-race-minded syndicated pair of Rowland Evans and Robert Novak regarded it as "a self-inflicted wound." Reagan then appeared to compound the error by simply choosing to appear at the evangelical Right's Religious Roundtable National Affairs Briefing at a Dallas arena, which featured plenty of red meat from figures like Jerry Falwell (who had just suggested that since President Carter had hired homosexuals, he should go ahead and hire murderers and bank robbers too). Reagan himself took the stage with one of his typical jokes: "You know, I've often had a fantasy: I've thought of serving an atheist a delicious gourmet dinner and then asking if he or she believed there was a cook." Such remarks were seen by some as pandering at best; at worst they seemed to betray a combination of contempt and ignorance that made him unfit for leadership of a pluralistic society.[3]

The conventional wisdom among the cognoscenti was that Reagan simply did not work. One *Times* columnist compared him with Barry Goldwater on the right in 1964 and George McGovern on the left in 1972, arguing that Reagan would show yet again the disaster that inevitably follows when the mainstream parties promote a fringe candidate.[4] Duke University political scientist James David Barber tacked in a somewhat different direction, seeing Reagan as not too radical, but rather lacking sufficient engagement to be an effective president. Barber, whose famed 1972 study *The Presidential Character* offered readers a taxonomy of executive types, speculated that Reagan would be feckless: sunny in disposition but lacking in the necessary vigor to be effective. "People frightened by Mr. Reagan's rhetoric should take comfort from the fact that he doesn't really mean it," Barber explained. "The right reason to worry about Mr. Reagan is his passive-positive character," he said, invoking one of his four categories (the other three were passive-negative; active-positive and active-negative—this last toxic combination attributed to the persona of the disgraced Richard Nixon). "It might be that Ronald Reagan will be just wonderful as president, perhaps presiding over a restorative national nap," Barber speculated with the air of condescension that so often hovered over those who underestimated Reagan (a perception which Reagan himself was happy to feed with lines like "I am concerned about what's happening in government—and it's cost me many a sleepless afternoon").[5] But it should be said that Barber's analysis was prescient in anticipating the biggest failure of his presidency, the Iran-Contra Scandal, where the most charitable assessment of Reagan's performance was that he was asleep at the wheel.

There were more objective metrics working in Carter's favor. New numbers in late summer showed that inflation was leveling off for the first time in thirteen years. Consumer confidence was edging up. The news on Wall Street was encouraging.[6] If the economy—often the key measure of a presidential candidate's prospects—turned a corner, maybe Carter could finally break away and win reelection.

But in 1980, perhaps more so than in other years up to that point, perceptions seemed to matter more than reality. And in this arena, Reagan was gaining momentum. Carter had spent much of the year trying to stay above the fray; this Rose Garden strategy, as it was known, was good politics as well as a reflection of Carter's task-oriented temperament. But as summer gave way to fall, Carter's team decided he really needed to take the gloves off—something that may have been easier for him to do, because he was both appalled and angry that an opponent he regarded as second-rate had a real chance of defeating him. Campaign chairman Robert Strauss publicly questioned whether Reagan was "a man of presidential caliber." Carter himself, in a speech from Martin Luther King Jr.'s former pulpit in Atlanta on September 16, noted that Reagan had appeared in Neshoba County, Mississippi, the previous month and had spoken approvingly of states' rights in a thinly veiled appeal to racist whites in an attempt to break the Democratic hold of the South. "You've seen the stirrings of hate," Carter said, adding that "Racism has no place in this country." But the strategy backfired; whatever legitimacy there may have been to such assertions, an implication of racism was regarded as a very serious charge that no responsible adult should make lightly. Since Reagan had not made any *explicitly* racist remarks, coverage instead focused on Carter's "meanness," a sense that the genial Georgian of 1976 had been replaced by an aggrieved and exhausted incumbent four years later. Hugh Sidey, a *Time* columnist whose beat was the presidency, noted that "the past few days have revealed a man of far more petty vituperation than most Americans thought possible even in a mean political season."[7]

Meanwhile, for all his lapses in language and judgment—and all too clear dog whistles to hate—it was becoming increasingly clear that Reagan, in the words of Brown University historian James Patterson, "was a formidable political figure. Despite his age, he remained a graceful, athletic, physically fit man who seemed far younger than sixty-nine. He had a marvelously soothing baritone and an easy platform manner, and was a captivating public presence and speaker."[8] More than that, Reagan was increasingly viewed as a leader. A *Times/CBS* poll in September revealed that "far more Americans believe that Ronald Reagan has a vision of the nation's future and the ability to lead it than those who see such qualities in President Carter." The poll did show that Carter was considered more attuned to the needs of ordinary people than Reagan, and less likely to start a war. But it also suggested they believed the economy would improve under Reagan. Analysts that month still saw the race as very close, though the demographics of the battleground states—in those days, they included California, New York, and Texas alongside more durably familiar ones like Michigan, Pennsylvania, and Florida—did suggest a tilt toward Reagan. This perception held fast into early October, even as observers did not regard it as static.[9]

As the race headed into its final month, three key dynamics were seen as critical. The first, as noted, was the economy. The second was the outcome of any televised presidential debates. The third was the fate of the hostages in Iran.

It is important to keep in mind that presidential debates in 1980 were not as tightly stitched into the fabric of the nation's political culture as they would become in the decades that followed. The first television debates, of course, had taken place between Richard Nixon and John F. Kennedy in 1960. They were seen as an attempt to resurrect the high-mindedness of the Senate debates between Abraham Lincoln and Stephen Douglas in 1858 (which were anything but). Notwithstanding such precedent, the Nixon–Kennedy debates were notable for their modernity: they demonstrated the power of television in shaping political perception, and as such were seen as critical in Kennedy gaining credibility as a leader in the eyes of the electorate. But the debates went dormant after that; there weren't any in 1964, 1968, or 1972, before they were resurrected in 1976 for a pair of debates between Carter and Gerald Ford (and one between vice presidential candidates Walter Mondale and Robert Dole), most remembered today for Ford's misstatement that Poland was not under Soviet domination, though how much difference such gaffes make is always a question.[10] Ironically—or perhaps inevitably given the power of incumbency—Carter, who had been the beneficiary of debates in 1976, was not eager to return to them in 1980, because he didn't want to give Reagan legitimacy and feared that Anderson, who was polling well enough to be plausibly included, seemed likely to cut into his support. ("Once you start opening up the system, it is hard to say where you draw the line," said spokesman Jody Powell; Carter had also refused to debate Ted Kennedy).[11] The wrangling over terms started in the spring and extended into the fall; Reagan and Anderson had a civil debate without Carter in Baltimore in September, which didn't have any obvious outcome beyond a drop in support for Anderson, which would likely have happened anyway, given the history of third-party candidates in American history. The League of Women Voters, which sponsored the contests, finally got Carter and Reagan to agree on a single presidential debate to be held on October 28, 1980—by any measure, the climax of the campaign.

Meanwhile, the contest ground on. A cartoon in the Charlotte *News* showed Reagan and Carter as school boys in front of a blackboard. Reagan, smiling while holding chalk, had written "$2 + 2 = 22$." Carter, beaming with a slide rule, had converted the equation into a complex multivariable formula that began and ended with the result that "$2 + 2 = 2 + 2$."[12] It was a brilliant encapsulation of what frustrated many voters about their choice.

Each candidate tried to alleviate his own weaknesses. In a speech in Michigan on October 1, Carter noted that it was he, a Democrat—not a corporate-minded Republican—who had stepped in to help Chrysler when the automaker faced its hour of crisis in the wake of the energy crisis and foreign competition. Reagan, condemned by the National Organization of Women for his "medieval stance on women's issues," promised that if elected he would appoint a woman to the Supreme Court (a promise he kept with Sandra Day O'Connor in 1981). A *Times*/CBS poll published on October 23 showed the race as a tie, with each candidate hovering around 40 percent, and Anderson falling to a plateau of 10 percent.[13]

The two finally had their one and only showdown in Cleveland a week before Election Day. Carter by that point was champing at the bit to get at Reagan. He and his team "presumed the public would see what he saw," Rick Perlstein later reported in his massive study of the campaign. "Which was that Carter was smart and Reagan was stupid. And that therefore Reagan would lose the debate." Yet, as Perlstein noted, Reagan had performed well in every major public debate in which he had participated. After one such joust with Robert F. Kennedy on the Vietnam War in 1967, Kennedy yelled, "Who the fuck got me into this?" and ordered aides never to pair him with "that son-of-a-bitch" again.[14]

The mistake Reagan's opponents repeatedly made is that they believed facts were determinative—that they spoke for themselves and that getting caught in a contradiction would be fatal. But Reagan, as he shown over the course of the 1980 campaign, was operating on another level, a realm of myth where belief functioned as a kind of self-actualizing truth. So it was, for example, that Carter, in laying out a detailed proposal for health care reform, noted that Reagan had begun his political career in the early sixties opposing Medicaid and Medicare. This was an accurate assertion—Reagan had repeatedly labeled such programs as "socialized medicine"—and, given the enormous popularity of Medicare in particular, such opinions could be seen as a serious blow to his credibility. And yet the TV cameras showed Reagan bearing an expression of patient amusement as he waited to reply. That reply, "There you go again," was delivered more in sorrow than in anger. Reagan went on to explain that it wasn't that he opposed Medicare, but that he favored another proposal, one which he never named and one which he was never subsequently asked about. This was an early illustration of why Congresswoman Patricia Schroeder of Colorado would later describe Reagan as "the Teflon president": nothing ever really seemed to stick to him (an analogy that came to her while she was making eggs). Carter's own attempt to be personable, an anecdote about a conversation he had with his thirteen-year-old daughter Amy, was widely seen as falling flat—cloying or absurd. By contrast, Reagan's slip in his closing remarks—thanking the good people of Cleveland for their hospitality "during the last moments of my life"—was overlooked. More remembered was a closing question that would be much talked about and remembered: "Are you better off than you were four years ago?" The query, subsequently blasted in caps in a one-page ad, would remain an important barometer of presidential races for decades to come.[15]

There was widespread consensus that Reagan had won the debate. Internal polling showed that in response to the question of whether he was a strong leader, a positive answer jumped from 42 to 61 percent. Republicans were particularly taken with a joke Reagan was telling: "A recession is when your neighbor loses his job, and a depression is when you lose your job." A pause, and then: "A recovery is when Jimmy Carter loses his." (Another favorite: "Government is like a baby, an alimentary canal at one end and no sense of responsibility on the other.") And yet, for all Reagan's appeal, polls published over the weekend before Election Day on Tuesday, November 4, showed the race as even.[16]

Meanwhile, the fate of the fifty-two hostages loomed large as the race reached its climax. The crisis had dominated headlines at the start of the year but had largely receded after the failed rescue attempt in April. Now there was a steady stream of stories—many of them speculative or uncorroborated—that began to bubble to the surface. Each campaign was convinced that the other was dabbling in subterfuge—planning an "October surprise," a phrase that entered the nation's political lexicon.[17] However, no one really knew anything, because Iranian politics, as they had been all year, were too volatile to say with any certainty what was, or would be, happening. On October 29, the Iranian parliament, or Majlis, announced that it would hold a public session to discuss the status of the hostages. On October 30, a high-ranking judge said that the government's goal was to free them before the American election, resulting in a protest that prevented a quorum in the chamber. Because October 31 was a Muslim holy day, confusion continued into the new month, when deliberations got under way during the weekend of November 1–2. The Reagan team prepared remarks in the event the hostages would be freed, but Sunday came and went without resolution. Carter broke into a football broadcast to say "I wish I could predict when the hostages will return. I cannot." Walter Cronkite of CBS, the most prestigious news anchor in a nation still stitched together by network TV, ended his show on Tuesday, November 4, by playing what had become the nation's unofficial anthem, Tony Orlando and Dawn's 1973 hit "Tie a Yellow Ribbon Round the Ole

Oak Tree" (bearing yellow ribbons commemorating the hostages had become a national ritual). Election Day happened to mark the one-year anniversary of the crisis.[18]

Considered against the wider context of U.S. history, the presidential election of 1980 was a somewhat odd one. Barely half the electorate chose to cast a ballot, the lowest turnout since 1948.[19] And yet it was a seesaw contest for its entire run, with no clear favorite on Election Day, giving the contest a real sense of drama. This made for another surprise: the outcome was not close. Reagan won a majority, albeit a narrow one, of 50.7 percent. Carter garnered only 41 percent of the vote, with most of the rest going to Anderson (6.6 percent). But the contest was a wipeout in the Electoral College: Reagan won 489 votes to Carter's 49 (the incumbent won only Rhode Island, Maryland, West Virginia, Hawaii, Mondale's home state of Minnesota and his own of Georgia, and Washington, DC).[20] It was, arguably, a landslide election.

Less arguably, 1980 marked a realignment. This was not only a matter of a new ideological force taking the presidency, but also a shift in Congress. The House of Representatives remained Democratic, as it had been since 1954, but the GOP gained thirty-three seats. More striking were the results in the U.S. Senate, where Republican membership jumped from forty-one to fifty-three, giving the GOP control of the chamber for the first time since 1955. A series of liberal lions—Frank Church of Idaho, Birch Bayh of Indiana, and George McGovern of South Dakota, the Democratic nominee for president in 1972—were defeated. For the first time since Herbert Hoover, who ran in 1932 during the very depths of the Great Depression, an elected incumbent was denied a bid for reelection. There was no question that a new day was dawning in Washington, DC.

Not everyone was on board with the new order. Carter retained a hold with African Americans, union members, and low-income voters in cities. The race was also notable for an emerging divide in American politics: the gender gap. Reagan narrowly won the women's vote, 46 percent to 45 percent for Carter. But 54 percent of men backed Reagan, while only 37 percent went for Carter. In years to come, the Democrats would increasingly become a party of women.[21] It would also become even more decisively the party of African Americans; Carter took 93 percent of their votes, while Reagan got 71 percent of those who most strongly opposed government efforts on behalf of black people. For political scientists Thomas and Mary Edsall, 1980 marked the crystallization of a racially based white politics that had been building since the mid-sixties, one that they would chronicle in their influential study *Chain Reaction*.[22]

There were other surprises. A *Times* / CBS poll published on November 6 revealed that about 20 percent of voters changed their minds in the last four days of the race, most of them going to Reagan. The Iranian hostage crisis loomed large in their minds (although those who considered it the *most* important issue went with Carter), as did growing unhappiness with the incumbent's handling of the economy. Carter focused on reducing inflation in part because his team believed that it was a major preoccupation for voters, though it turned out that they were more worried about unemployment, and most of those people went for Reagan, whose probusiness policies would presumably create jobs. Eighty-four percent of Reagan voters gave "time for a change" as a reason for choosing him—which was less a matter of explicit ideology than a more generalized sense of unhappiness with the state of the country. Those who considered U.S. stature in the world their most important issue went decisively for Reagan. So did white evangelical Christians; Carter had taken two-thirds of them in 1976; Reagan got 61 percent of their vote four years later. It was the beginning of a decades-long love affair between social and religious conservatives. Lou Harris was the only pollster who had predicted a Reagan victory. He was also the only one closely measuring the impact of the Christian Right.[23]

Carter knew he had lost the election ninety minutes after the first ballots were counted. He was on *Air Force One*, and was in tears when told "it's all over" by his staff. He wanted to concede immediately, but was advised to wait until 2 a.m., when the tide was unmistakable. "I promised you four years ago, that I would never lie to you, so I can't stand here tonight and tell you it doesn't hurt," he told supporters. Carter was gracious and dignified in pledging a seamless transition and in affirming the majesty of the democratic process, and in extending special thanks to Walter Mondale. He would go back to work, diligently as ever, and work through the night on Inauguration Day.[24]

He didn't want to have any unfinished business at the end of an era.

FIGURE 15. President Ronald Reagan addresses partygoers assembled in the Rotunda of the National Museum of Natural History, one of nine official balls held to celebrate his presidency on the evening of January 20, 1981. Mrs. Reagan is at his side. Noted for its glamour—some said excess—Reagan's inauguration marked a turning point in American history comparable to that of Thomas Jefferson in 1801, Andrew Jackson in 1829, and Donald Trump in 2017. (Smithsonian Institution Archives)

Conclusion

Inaugurating the Eighties

THE MOST NOTORIOUS PRESIDENTIAL inauguration of the nineteenth century took place on March 4, 1829. Andrew Jackson had been elected president four months earlier. Four years earlier, after a complex series of machinations in the House of Representatives, Jackson had been denied the office despite winning the popular vote, and his partisans clung fast to their man, making the presidency of the victor in that race, John Quincy Adams, as miserable as possible (which was pretty miserable indeed, especially since JQA, as he was known, was something of a melancholy figure to begin with). Now Jackson's champions had prevailed in a rematch, and their man was in the White House. And so were they—in a party for the ages. An estimated 20,000 well-wishers made their way to the celebration, most of them uninvited and many of them wearing coonskin caps in tribute to the Tennessean, the first man to be elected from the western frontier. Liquor flowed freely; furniture was trashed. Jackson himself slipped out of the festivities on horseback and spent his first night in office at a local hotel. Over the course of the next eight years, Jackson would be one of the most polarizing figures in American history—and still is. But few would dispute that his presidency marked a new chapter in American history.[1]

The most notorious presidential inauguration of the twentieth century took place on January 20, 1981. However, this was for entirely different reasons. When Jimmy Carter took office four years earlier, he made a point of walking from the U.S. Capitol to the White House in a democratic gesture reminiscent of Thomas Jefferson, who had done the same in 1801. Ronald Reagan's coterie had a different approach. So many corporate jets were parked at Washington's National Airport that there was no room for private planes. Limousines were requisitioned from as far away as Atlanta and New York; a group of Indiana Republicans arrived by train in a railroad car once owned by J. P. Morgan. The elite catering firm of Ridgewells served 400,000 hors d'oeuvres during preinaugural parties. First Lady Nancy Reagan wore a hand-sewn, beaded gown estimated to cost $25,000—critics noted it would buy a year's supply of food stamps for fifty needy citizens—and a handbag that cost $1600. Johnny Carson, who attended the event, described it as "the first administration to have a premiere."[2]

While there were those who found the affair excessive to the point of grotesque, some ordinary Americans took heart in the spectacle. "I got laid off at Ford last week," an autoworker told a *Washington Post* reporter while standing on the inaugural parade route. "I spent the last money that I have for entertainment to come down here today. I just wanted to see what Reagan had to say." The pregnant wife of a couple who had traveled from Illinois explained, "We're going to call our baby, Ronnie, because we want him to always remember that he was named for a great American. I think the country is really about to turn around."[3]

That was certainly something that Reagan was promising. His inaugural address clearly sounded a new note in the most famous line in his inaugural address: "In this present crisis, government is not the solution to our problem; government is the problem." More broadly, he cast the nation's economic situation in starkly libertarian terms: "These United States are confronted with an economic affliction of great proportions. We suffer from the longest and one of the worst sustained inflations in our national history. It distorts our economic decisions, penalizes thrift, and crushes the struggling young and the fixed-income elderly alike. It threatens to shatter the lives of millions of our people. Idle industries have cast workers into unemployment, causing human misery and personal indignity. Those who do work are denied a fair return for their labor by a tax system which penalizes successful achievement and keeps us from maintaining full productivity." But Reagan ended on an affirmative note. He cited a letter he had recently read about a World War I veteran, Martin Treptow, who, before dying in France, had made a pledge: "America must win this war. Therefore I will work, I will save, I will sacrifice, I will endure, I will fight cheerfully and do my utmost, as if the issue of the whole struggle depended on me alone." Reagan concluded by saying, "The crisis we are facing today does not require of us the kind of sacrifice that Martin Treptow and so many thousands of others were called upon to make. It does require, however, our best effort, and our willingness to believe in ourselves and to believe in our capacity to perform great deeds; to believe that together, with God's help, we can and will resolve the problems which now confront us.

"And, after all, why shouldn't we believe that?" he concluded rhetorically. We are Americans. God bless you, and thank you."[4]

Why shouldn't we, indeed. Here and at other times in the years that followed, Reagan's words seemed to generate self-fulfilling prophecy. President Carter had spent the final sleepless hours of his presidency working feverishly to secure the release of the American hostages in Iran before he left office. "Did you get a look at Carter?" a shocked Reagan asked aide Michael Deaver when the outgoing and incoming presidents met at the White House on the morning of Inauguration Day. Reagan, of course, looked like a million dollars; Carter was an ashen wreck who still had not shaved at 10:45 a.m. (About four hours earlier, Carter had called Reagan to give him the news that the hostages' release was imminent, only to be informed that Reagan was asleep and not to be disturbed.) A typical series of delays followed—there were wrangles about unfreezing Iranian banking assets, and perhaps, a desire to administer one last jab to the Carter administration—and the plane with the hostages did not actually take off until 12:25 p.m. Washington time, after Reagan was officially president. Jimmy Carter could not escape the Iran hostage crisis; Reagan would not have to deal with it. Somehow that seemed typical of Reagan's past and future penchant for sidestepping responsibility.[5]

Certainly, there were signs the country was ready to turn the page. Though the nation was still grieving the loss of John Lennon in January 1981, his upbeat number-one song, "(Just Like) Starting Over," was perhaps ironically apt. At the box office, 9 to 5 was riding high, as was Dallas in the Nielsen ratings, and Carl Sagan's Cosmos was on the bestseller lists—all works, however varied, that were marked by good cheer, whatever social critiques they were (or weren't) making. Indeed, it wouldn't take long—well before the decade was over, in fact—for "the eighties" to become a byword for optimism, prosperity, and patriotism in American society.

Of course, it wasn't that simple. The coming decade brought all kinds of challenges to all kinds of people, whether those struggling with the AIDS crisis (just coming into view in 1981) or the crack epidemic that infested the nation's cities in the coming decade. The suffering was also more general; those who lived through the period sometimes forget that the economic recession of 1981–1982 was the worst the nation had experienced since the Great Depression, and that it dogged Reagan's popularity, much as the inflationary woes that had underlaid the contraction had dogged his predecessor. That recession also sparked two classic works of popular culture in the form of Bruce Springsteen's Nebraska—a chilling portrait of a spiritual no less than economic crisis in the nation's heartland—and Billy Joel's The Nylon Curtain, a valediction to the fading postwar generation of suburbanites. Both were released in 1982.

Perhaps the starkest reminder that the shadows of recent history still loomed occurred on March 30, 1981, when Reagan—like a series of presidents before him—was the target of an assassination attempt. He survived, but a good deal more narrowly than was commonly understood at the time, in part because of Reagan's exceptionally good cheer ("Honey, I forgot to duck," he told his wife Nancy as he was wheeled into the emergency room).[6] This bought him the good will that helped him win passage of his 1981 economic program. But in the eyes of some observers, Reagan was never the same after that, as some of the jokes about his disengagement appeared to veer a little closer to reality.

By the mid-eighties, though, that no longer seemed to matter. The economy recovered, and a buoyant new mood captured much of the country, reflected in Reagan's 1984 reelection campaign theme: "It's morning in America." Tellingly, even some of the skeptics seemed to agree. Joel followed *The Nylon Curtain* in 1983 with *An Innocent Man*, an infectious collection of pop songs that paid tribute to the earlier generation of artists who had inspired him. Springsteen followed up *Nebraska* in 1984 with *Born in the U.S.A.*, a full-tilt rock record that turned him into a durable cultural icon. While Springsteen's work has always been too dappled to be characterized as simply happy or sad—the title track of the album, about a Vietnam veteran struggling with post-traumatic stress disorder was widely mischaracterized as a patriotic anthem—it is nevertheless not entirely inaccurate to assert that an embrace of tradition and national pride also threads through his work, and that the tens of millions of listeners who bought it, literally and figuratively, were not misguided in doing so.

Still, if, in the words of a common slogan at the time, America was back, it wasn't back in quite the same way. The United States in the 1980s was quite literally a nation on borrowed time. Because of the constellation of power in Washington, where a Republican president faced off against a still largely Democratic Congress, Reagan's tax cuts were not offset by cuts in spending, and the two sides settled on a tacit agreement that the difference would be made up with fiscal deficits, beginning a long chain of debt that extends to the present day and which is unlikely to be without lasting consequences. Reagan wasn't kidding when he told his fellow Americans that they would not be required to make big sacrifices. Though an ascendant religious conservatism placed new emphasis on moral behavior, capitalism has always fostered some degree of self-gratification in the form of consumption, and the eighties were nothing if not an age that celebrated the fruits of prosperity, earned or not.

Similarly, the nation's military power remained immense, but it continued to face challenges. The Cold War wasn't over, and in the short term, at least, there were widespread fears at home and abroad that the new turn toward hostility between the superpowers after the Soviet invasion of Afghanistan would worsen in the Reagan years, especially given the new administration's evident desire to achieve nuclear superiority. By decade's end it was clear that the United States would prevail. But in the meantime, new threats, especially in the form of terrorism and rising fundamentalist extremism, were intensifying as a problem. No serious observer on the planet believed that the nation was as powerful in 1985 as it had been in 1945.

Economics and military power aside, there were also questions about the promise of America itself as the nation entered the new decade. One of the more notable books to be published in 1980 was that of radio talk show host and ethnographer Studs Turkel, whose latest collection of oral histories, *American Dreams: Lost and Found*, received a glowing review on the front page of the *New York Times Book Review* in September of that year. Reviewer Robert Sherrill called *American Dreams* "a dark-hued book of frustrations and disillusionment, but it also is a stirringly hopeful book," noting the evident resilience of its subjects. One of those subjects, a sixteen-year-old high school student named Linda Haas, captured the sense of unease that seemed to accompany what passed for prosperity: "I think that for my father and his generation, the dream was to have a home and security and things like that. It was because of the poverty they came from. I don't know what it is now. The kids I go to school with [she was attending a large technical school], when they talk about their dreams, they don't talk about a home or having money in the bank. It's more like trying to have personal satisfaction. They don't know what they want. I don't know what I want." An aspiring folk singer made a similar observation: "There's a terrible mobility in this society. It's too easy to run away from things. The ease with which you can shift your ground makes the ground fall away from you all the time."[7]

The view was similarly unsettled at the top. "My good friend Milton Friedman says the worst thing is for businessmen to feel responsible to society," Gaylord Freeman, chairman of the First National

Bank of Chicago, told Terkel. "He says that's a lot of baloney and it's contrary to the businessman's assignment. It's an arrogance he should not have. I don't accept that, though I greatly admire Friedman."[8] In the years that followed, Friedman's perspective became increasingly dominant, as shareholder value displaced considerations of workers or the communities at large as the primary consideration for any corporation. Friedman, it should be noted, was not a heartless capitalist; indeed, he was an early articulator and cheerleader for a universal basic income, an idea that now has a strong progressive valence. But that wasn't, or isn't, the primary thing he was known for. Instead, he was known as the architect of the kind of libertarian-minded economics that became the prevailing common sense of the decade—and beyond.

Indeed, while the United States may have been on borrowed time in the 1980s, that spending bought something tangible: a sense of social stability. Reagan left office in 1989, on the eve of the fall of the Berlin Wall, and American triumph in the Cold War, which left the nation as the lone superpower on the planet. Reagan's hand-picked successor, George H. W. Bush, presided over what was essentially Reagan's third term. Even when Democrat Bill Clinton took over in 1993, the governing logic of the eighties—captured in Clinton's famous 1995 line that "the era of big government is over"—continued straight on into the twenty-first century. Not until 9/11, the War on Terror, and the financial crisis of 2008 did the long glow of the eighties finally begin to fade. The election of Barack Obama brought hope that a new day was dawning, but few Americans today feel much confidence that that was actually true.

The most notorious presidential inauguration of the twenty-first century took place on January 20, 2017. As with Andrew Jackson's inauguration 188 years earlier, this one was a populist uprising of sorts (it was followed four years later with a much more ominous literal uprising). As with Reagan's inauguration 36 years earlier, the 2017 one was also marked by a sense of opulence reflecting the fact that Donald J. Trump was an unabashed capitalist with no previous government experience. But while Jackson's and Reagan's inaugurations were animated by a sense of hope, however controversial, Trump's was marked by fears on both the Left and the Right, as reflected in the "American carnage" he cited in his inaugural speech. In the years that followed, the Republican Party over which Trump presided had less and less connection—temperamentally or philosophically—with the party of Reagan and the wave of change he represented. That day, the day 1980 inaugurated, is now yesterday.

ACKNOWLEDGMENTS

IN 1980, I was in high school. It was in that year that I was appointed editor-in-chief of my school newspaper (for which I would later be cited as New York State Student Journalist of the Year, even though subsequent events would demonstrate that I lacked the requisite skills to be a reporter). So it is with a sense of a circle closing that I return to this year as a matter of memory and history, the former rapidly giving way to the latter.

A few words of thanks are in order:

I'm grateful for the opportunity to work again with the talented staff of Rutgers University Press. This includes my editor, (and editorial director) Kimberly Guinta; sales and marketing director Jeremy Grainger; and publicity director Courtney Brach. I owe a particular debt to editorial director Kim for rescuing me when I steered into some shoals. Thanks also to copyeditor Diane Ersepke of Miccinello Associates, who went over the manuscript with a fine-toothed comb, and designer Dave Kessler, who designed the evocative cover, for their work on my behalf.

I've benefited, as I have a number of times now, from a thoroughly informed and insightful reading from William Norman, who saved me from countless errors and provided me with valuable insights. My wife, Lyde Sizer, and her student, Michael Nathanson, also gave the manuscript a valuable vetting. Wally Levis remained a stalwart friend and counselor. I'd also like to thank my agent, Roger Williams of the Roger Williams Agency, for his help with this project.

As work on this book was getting under way amid the COVID pandemic of 2020–2022, I began a new job at the newly founded upper division at Greenwich Country Day School. I savor the company and support of my colleagues, notably Adam Rohdie, Chris Winters, Andrew Ruoss, and Lauren Waller. Having such a firm institutional foundation has made sustaining my scholarly passions possible for a little while longer. My thanks to all in the GCDS community.

This book, like a number of previous ones, was substantially written at the Starbucks coffee shop in Dobbs Ferry, New York. I was gladdened by the proficiency and good will of the staff there and the camaraderie of a community that buoyed me for much of the last decade.

My family continues to be my mainstay source of sustenance, even as the lives of my four children—Jay, Gray, Ry, and Nancy—continue to take on distinctive contours. My wife, Lyde, remains by my side. My final words of thanks are, again, to her.

Jim Cullen
Hastings-on-Hudson, New York
April 2022

NOTES

Introduction

1. Rick Perlstein, *Reaganland: America's Right Turn, 1976–1980* (New York: Simon & Schuster, 2020). Other installments, chronologically, are *Before the Storm: Barry Goldwater and the Unmaking of American Consensus* (New York: Hill & Wang, 2001); *Nixonland: The Rise of a President and the Fracturing of America* (New York: Simon & Schuster, 2008); and *The Invisible Bridge: The Fall of Nixon and the Rise of Reagan* (New York: Simon & Schuster, 2014).

2. Clinton made this remark in his State of the Union Address of January 23, 1996, https://clintonwhitehouse4.archives.gov/WH/New/other/sotu.html.

Chapter 1   On the Cusp

1. Eric Pace, "U.S. Embassy in Iran Advises Departure of All Dependents"; *New York Times*, January 1, 1979, 1, Fox Butterfield, "Pro-U.S. Mood Is a Revolution for the Chinese"; *New York Times*, January 1, 1979, 1, Bernadine Morris, "Will the Retro Look Make It?" *New York Times*, January 1, 1979, 18.

2. For an excellent treatment of the reorientation of Chinese communism in the late 1978, see Christian Caryl, *Strange Rebels: 1979 and the Birth of the 21st Century* (repr., New York: Basic, 2014), 117–135.

3. Dani Matias, "U.S. Women with College Degrees Could Soon Be the Majority of Workers," National Public Radio, June 20, 2019, https://www.npr.org/2019/06/20/734408574/new-report-says-college-educated-women-will-soon-make-up-majority-of-u-s-labor-f.

4. Gene Maeroff, "Colleges, Facing Declines, Advised to Lure Students, *New York Times*, January 1, 1979, A6; Center for Education Statistics, Office of

Educational Research and Improvement, U.S. Department of Education, "Growth in Higher Education Enrollment, 1978–1985," 1986, https://www.cia .gov/library/readingroom/docs/CIA-RDP90-00530R000300620012-3.pdf; "Hot Offices Burning Up Federal Workers," *New York Times*, January 1, 1979, A6.

5. Peter N. Carroll, *It Seemed Like Nothing Happened: America in the 1970s* (1982; New Brunswick, NJ: Rutgers University Press, 1990); Christopher B. Strain, *The Long Sixties: America, 1955–1973* (Malden, MA: Wiley Blackwell, 2016); Bruce J. Schulman, *The Seventies: The Great Shift in American Culture, Society and Politics* (New York: Da Capo, 2001); Edward Berkowitz, *Something Happened: A Political and Cultural Overview of the Seventies* (New York: Columbia University Press, 2005); David Frum, *How We Got Here: The 70s, The Decade That Brought You Modern Life—for Better or Worse* (New York: Basic Books, 2000); Philip Jenkins, *Decade of Nightmares: The End of the Sixties and the Making of Eighties America* (New York: Oxford University Press, 2008).

6. Todd Gitlin, *The Sixties: Years of Hope, Days of Rage* (1997; New York: Bantam, 1993).

7. Andreas Hillen, *1973 Nervous Breakdown: Watergate, Warhol, and the Birth of Post-Sixties America* (repr.; New York: Bloomsbury, 2006).

8. Ronald Brownstein, *Rock Me on the Water: 1974—the Year Los Angeles Transformed Movies, Television and Politics* (New York: Harper, 2021). The title of this fine study is a bit of a misnomer, in that Brownstein's study essentially runs from about 1967 to 1977 (indeed, the Jackson Browne song of its title was released in 1972), but the larger point remains the same: the seventies were an exciting time for some.

9. Tom Wolfe, "The Me Decade and the Third Great Awakening," *New York Magazine*, August 23, 1976, https://nymag.com/news/features/45938/.

10. Much of the following is derived from Jim Cullen, *Democratic Empire: The United States since 1945* (Malden, MA: Wiley-Blackwell, 2017), 168–169. For a more detailed examination of the evangelical Christianity in this period, see Steven P. Miller, *The Age of Evangelicalism: American's Born-Again Years* (New York: Oxford University Press 2014). One of the more notable scholars on the subject is Frances Fitzgerald. See her portrait of Falwell in *Cities on a Hill: A Brilliant Exploration of Visionary Communities Remaking the American Dream* (New York: Simon & Schuster, 1986) and *The Evangelicals: The Struggle to Reshape America* (New York: Simon & Schuster, 2017).

11. Jerry Falwell, excerpt from *Listen, America!* (New York: Doubleday, 1980) included in *The United States Since 1945: A Documentary Reader*, ed. Robert P. Ingalls and David K. Johnson (Malden, MA: Wiley-Blackwell, 2009), 173, 176.

12. Alex Cohen and Wilfred U. Codrington III, *The Equal Rights Amendment Explained*, Brennan Center for Justice, January 23, 2020, https://www.brennan center.org/our-work/research-reports/equal-rights-amendment-explained.

13. Miller, *The Age of Evangelicalism*, 43.

14. Kevin Mattson, *What the Heck Are You Up To, Mr. President? Jimmy Carter, America's "Malaise" and the Speech That Should Have Changed the Country* (New York: Bloomsbury, 2009). The text of the speech is included as an appendix (the quotes here come from pp. 210–211); for the initial and subsequent reaction, see 159–166.

15. For a good study of the energy crisis, see Meg Jacobs, *Panic at the Pump: The Energy Crisis and the Transformation of American Politics in the 1970s* (New York: Hill & Wang, 2016). Rick Perlstein describes the confusion and frustration surrounding the 1979 gas lines in *Reaganland: America's Right Turn, 1976–1980* (New York: Simon & Schuster, 2020), 556–568.

16. Jon Ward, *Camelot's End: Kennedy vs. Carter and the Fight That Broke the Democratic Party* (New York: Twelve, 2019). The facts surrounding Chappaquid-dick are discussed on pp. 68–70; Kennedy's frustration with the "Malaise Speech" is noted on p. 142 ("It was in the aftershocks of this speech that I began thinking seriously about running for the presidency in 1980," Ward records him as saying.)

17. Ward, 125; Perlstein, *Reaganland*, 653.

18. The standard history of New Hollywood is Peter Biskind's now classic *Easy Riders, Raging Bulls: How the Sex-Drugs-and-Rock 'N' Roll Generation Saved Hollywood* (New York: Simon & Schuster, 1998).

19. Nielsen Media Research figures posted on Wikipedia, 1978, https://en .wikipedia.org/wiki/Top-rated_United_States_television_programs_of _1978%E2%80%9379.

20. Nielsen Media Research figures posted on Wikipedia, 1979, https://en .wikipedia.org/wiki/Top-rated_United_States_television_programs_of _1979%E2%80%9380.

21. CBS News, "Popular Products of 1979," accessed November 14, 2020, https://www.cbsnews.com/news/popular-products-of-1979/.

22. Adam Clymer, "Maine Republicans, in Informal Ballot, Give Bush a Victory," *New York Times*, November 4, 1979, https://timesmachine.nytimes.com /timesmachine/1979/11/04/issue.html.

23. The key video clip is available via the *Boston Globe*, "The Interview That Blindsided the Ted Kennedy Presidential Campaign," November 4, 1979, https://www.youtube.com/watch?v=e5TkhNWPspM. Ward devotes a chapter to the fiasco in *Camelot's End*, 158–177. See also Perlstein, *Reaganland*, 655–659.

24. On the immediate circumstances of the embassy takeover, see Caryl, *Strange Rebels*, 229–230; and Perlstein, *Reaganland*, 636–646.

25. Caryl, 234; Perlstein, 647.

26. Much of the background here draws on Stephen Tanner, *Afghanistan: A Military History from Alexander the Great to the War against the Taliban*, rev. ed. (2002; New York: Da Capo, 2009), see esp. 227–238.

27. Quoted in Perlstein, *Reaganland*, 700.

Chapter 2   Wind Shear

1. On Reagan's propensity for embellishment while announcing Cubs games, see Garry Wills, *Reagan's America* (repr.; New York: Penguin, 1987), 127–131.

2. Lou Cannon, "Actor, Governor, President, Icon (Reagan Obituary)," *Washington Post*, June 6, 2004, https://www.washingtonpost.com/wp-dyn /articles/A18329-2004Jun5.html.

3. James Cannon, *Time and Chance: Gerald Ford's Appointment with History* (1994; Ann Arbor: University of Michigan Press, 1998), 292–294.

4. "Reagan, Spare That Tree!" *Washington Post*, August 17, 1980, https://www .washingtonpost.com/archive/opinions/1980/08/17/reagan-spare-that-tree /fcb1657a-6987-44f3-86c4-89daa1409fb1/; Josh Levin, "The Welfare Queen," *Slate*, December 13, 2013, http://www.slate.com/articles/news_and_politics /history/2013/12/linda_taylor_welfare_queen_ronald_reagan_made_her_a _notorious_american_villain.html; Rick Perlstein, *The Invisible Bridge: The Fall of Nixon and the Rise of Reagan* (New York: Simon & Schuster, 2014), 603–604.

5. Perlstein, *Invisible Bridge*, 250, 546.

6. Rick Perlstein renders a vivid rendition of the GOP convention in *The Invisible Bridge*. Numbers on Ford's deficit and Carter's victory are cited in Perlstein's successor volume, *Reaganland: America's Right Turn, 1976–1980* (New York: Simon & Schuster, 2020), 3.

7. You can see it on C-Span, accessed November 21, 2020, https://www.c -span.org/video/?324219-1/ronald-reagan-presidential-campaign -announcement.

8. Hedrick Smith, "Excluded from G.O.P. Debate, Four Rivals Attack Bush," *New York Times*, February 24, 1980, A1; Perlstein, *Reaganland*, 734–739.

9. Adam Clymer, "Ford Declares Reagan Can't Win; Invites G.O.P. to Ask Him to Run," *New York Times*, March 2, 1980, A1; Adam Clymer, "Ford Declines Race for the Presidency to Avoid G.O.P. Split," *New York Times*, March 16, 1980, A1.

10. "U.S. Hockey Team Defeats the Soviets in the 'Miracle on Ice,'" History .com, November 24, 2009, https://www.history.com/this-day-in-history/u-s -hockey-team-makes-miracle-on-ice. The event was memorialized in a 1981 television movie, *Miracle on Ice*, and the much more beloved 2004 film *Miracle*. For a book-length treatment, see Wayne Coffee, *The Boys of Winter: The Untold*

Story of a Coach, a Dream, and the 1980 U.S. Olympic Hockey Team (New York: Crown, 2005).

11. E. J. Dionne, "Previewing a Carter–Reagan Faceoff," *New York Times*, March 23, 1980, E3.

12. "Poll Finds Drop in Support for Carter in Iran Crisis," *New York Times*, January 11, 1980, A12; Robert A. Bennett, "Banks, Led by Chemical, Raise Prime Rate to 20%," *New York Times*, April 3, 1980, A1; Perlstein, *Reaganland*, 649, 762; James Reston, "Jimmy Carter's Luck, *New York Times*, February 29, 1980, A31.

13. Jon Ward, *Camelot's End: Kennedy vs. Carter and the Fight That Broke the Democratic Party* (New York: Twelve, 2019), 215–221.

14. Ward, 235.

15. Ward, 251.

16. Jim Cullen, *Democratic Empire: The United States since 1945* (Malden, MA: Wiley-Blackwell, 2017), 157; Steven P. Miller, *The Age of Evangelicalism: American's Born-Again Years* (New York: Oxford University Press 2014), 48-59.

17. Perlstein, *Reaganland*, 795–796.

18. Jon Meacham, *Destiny and Power: The American Odyssey of George Herbert Walker Bush* (New York: Random House, 2015), 248; Perlstein, *Reaganland*, 802–807.

19. Ward, *Camelot's End*, 266–273.

20. Adam Clymer, "Post Convention Polls: Quick Turnabout, as Usual," *New York Times*, August 20, 1980, A1.

21. Carey Winfrey, "Prospect of the Draft Gets a Mixed Reaction from Feminists," *New York Times*, January 29, 1980, A16; "Poll Finds U.S. Divided on Drafting of Women," *New York Times*, February 2, 1980, A7; National Organization for Women, position paper on "The Registration and Drafting of Women in 1980," December 2, 1980, https://ufdc.ufl.edu/AA00005244/00001/1j.

22. J. B. O'Mahoney, "Campus Women React to the Draft," *New York Times*, February 17, 1980, Westchester Weekly, 1; David Welna, "Time for Male-Only Draft Registration to Include Women, Says Panel," National Public Radio, March 25, 2020, https://www.npr.org/2020/03/25/821615322/commission-issues-verdict-women-like-men-should-have-to-sign-up-for-draft.

Chapter 3   The Closing of Heaven's Gate

1. Carson is alluding to a notorious 1973 incident when Marlon Brando, who won the Best Actor award for his performance in *The Godfather* and sent an Apache actor, Sacheen Littlefeather, to accept the award on his behalf, explaining that he "regretfully cannot accept this very generous award. And the reasons for this are the treatment of American Indians today by the film industry and on

television." According to a later account, Brando also cited the ongoing clash at Wounded Knee, where Native Americans exchanged gunfire with federal authorities for seventy-one days. See Tim Gray, "Oscar and Politics over the Decades, from Marlon Brando to Jimmy Kimmel," *Variety*, March 1, 2018, https://variety.com/2018/vintage/news/oscar-politics-controversy-marlon -brando-jimmy-kimmel-1202711409/.

2. For video clips from the ceremonies, including Carson's monologue, accessed January 4, 2021, see https://www.oscars.org/videos-photos/51st-oscars -highlights.

3. A brief history of *Apocalypse Now*'s production can be found at the American Film Institute website, accessed January 4, 2021, https://catalog.afi.com /Catalog/moviedetails/67464.

4. Steven Bach, *Final Cut: Dreams and Disaster in the Making of* Heaven's Gate (1985; New York: New American Library, 1987), 227. Bach notes that there were protesters outside the Pavilion, among them Vietnam Veterans Against the War.

5. Bach, 232-240.

6. On the rise of Hollywood as the nation's dream factory, see Thomas Schatz, *The Genius of the System: Hollywood Filmmaking in the Studio Era* (New York: Pantheon, 1988). Much of the discussion that follows draws on Jim Cullen, *A Short History of the Modern Media* (Malden, MA: Wiley Blackwell, 2014), 90-97.

7. The best single-volume treatment of New Hollywood is Peter Biskind's *Easy Riders, Raging Bulls: How the Sex-Drugs-and-Rock 'N' Roll Generation Saved Hollywood* (New York: Simon & Schuster, 1998). For a broad sampling of scholarship on the subject, see Thomas Elaesser, Alexander Horwath, and Noel King, eds., *The Last Great American Picture Show: New Hollywood Cinema in the Seventies* (Amsterdam: Amsterdam University Press, 2004). Much of what follows draws on Jim Cullen, *Democratic Empire: The United States Since 1945* (Malden, MA: Wiley-Blackwell, 2017), 127-128.

8. Tim Appelo, "Telluride: Francis Ford Coppola Spills 'Apocalypse Now' Secrets on 35th Anniversary," *Hollywood Reporter*, August 30, 2014, https://www .hollywoodreporter.com/news/telluride-francis-ford-coppola-spills-729281; Peter Cowie, *The Apocalypse Now Book* (New York: Da Capo, 2001), 124-125; Biskind, *Easy Riders*, 378.

9. Much of this history draws on Bach, *Final Cut*, chapters 1-3.

10. Bach, 77.

11. Bach, 122-126.

12. For an insightful reading of the role Rocky played in seventies popular culture, see Daniel J. Leab's essay, "The Blue Collar Ethnic in Bicentennial America: *Rocky*," in *Hollywood's America: Understanding History Through Film*,

5th ed., ed. Steven Mintz, Randy Roberts, and David Welky (Malden, MA: Blackwell-Wiley, 2016), 288–296.

13. Vincent LoBrutto, *Martin Scorsese: A Biography* (Westport, CT: Praeger, 2007), 222–223; Biskind, *Easy Riders*, 389–390; Bach, *Final Cut*, 171–174. Much of the following analysis of *Raging Bull* is derived from Jim Cullen, *Martin Scorsese and the American Dream* (New Brunswick, NJ: Rutgers University Press, 2021), xx.

14. The Wikipedia page for the film version of *The Shining* does a good job of surveying reaction to the film, accessed January 9, 2021, https://en.wikipedia.org/wiki/The_Shining_(film)#Initial_reviews.

15. The film finished in twelfth place according to The Numbers, a site where "data and the movie business meet," The Numbers, 1980, https://www.the-numbers.com/market/1980/top-grossing-movies.

16. The Numbers, 1980, https://www.the-numbers.com/market/1980/top-grossing-movies.

17. Robert Fink, "Prisoners of Pachelbel: An Essay in Post-Canonical Musicology," *Hamburg Jahrbuch*, 2010, https://www.academia.edu/581670/Prisoners_of_Pachelbel.

18. Aaron Latham, "The Ballad of the Urban Cowboy: America's Search for True Grit," *Esquire*, September 12, 1978, https://classic.esquire.com/article/1978/9/12/the-ballad-of-the-urban-cowboy-americas-search-for-true-grit.

19. Roger Cormier, "13 Fast Facts about *Smokey and the Bandit*," Mental Floss, May 27, 2017, https://www.mentalfloss.com/article/80484/13-fast-facts-about-smokey-and-bandit; Grosses are drawn from The Numbers website, accessed January 12, 2021, https://www.the-numbers.com/movie/Smokey-and-the-Bandit#tab=summary; https://www.the-numbers.com/box-office-records/domestic/all-movies/cumulative/released-in-1977; and https://www.the-numbers.com/market/1980/top-grossing-movies.

20. The review can be found at Ebert.com, accessed January 14, 2021, https://www.rogerebert.com/reviews/serial-1980.

21. The Numbers, accessed January 14, 2021, https://www.the-numbers.com/market/1980/top-grossing-movies; Sidney Lumet, *Making Movies* (New York: Vintage, 1996).

22. According to commentary accompanying the Amazon.com release of the film, the script was written by Nancy Meyers, Charles Shyer, and Harvey Miller. Meyers and Shyer, who were married, teamed up for a bunch of movies before their divorce, and Meyers struck off on her own as a successful director. The box office ranking comes from The Numbers, accessed January 14, 2021, https://www.the-numbers.com/market/1980/top-grossing-movies.

23. This information is included in the production trivia in the Amazon edition of the film.

24. Bach, *Final Cut*, 395.

25. Vincent Canby, "*Heaven's Gate*: A Western by Cimino," *New York Times*, November 19, 1980, nytimes.com: https://www.nytimes.com/1980/11/19/arts /heavens-gate-a-western-by-cimino.html.

26. Bach, *Final Cut*, 395–396, 407.

27. Bach, 396; Peter Brown, "Behind the *Heaven's Gate* Disaster," *Washington Post*, November 30, 1980, https://www.washingtonpost.com/archive/lifestyle /1980/11/30/behind-the-heavens-gate-disaster/632c5e49-df4a-4f6d-b669 -c730f87f4d1c/.

28. Manhola Dargis, "The Second Coming of *Heaven's Gate*," *New York Times*, March 17, 2013, https://www.nytimes.com/2013/03/17/movies/michael-ciminos -heavens-gate-returns-to-film-forum.html.

29. Bach cites this figure, which he notes can depend on how you calculate it, *Final Cut*, 459. The film took in about $3.5 million. See Seth Abramovitch, "Hollywood Flashback: *Heaven's Gate* Was Pulled from Theaters in 1980," *Hollywood Reporter*, November 21, 2020, https://www.hollywoodreporter.com /news/hollywood-flashback-heavens-gate-was-pulled-from-theaters-in-1980.

30. Abramovich.

31. Nicholas Barber, "*Heaven's Gate*: From Hollywood Disaster to Master-piece," BBC, December 4, 2015, https://www.bbc.com/culture/article/20151120 -heavens-gate-from-hollywood-disaster-to-masterpiece; BBC Culture, "The 100 greatest American Films": https://www.bbc.com/culture/article/20150720-the -100-greatest-american-films.

32. Roger Ebert, *Scorsese by Ebert* (Chicago: University of Chicago Press, 2009), 149.

33. Dargis, "The Second Coming."

34. Academy of Motion Pictures Arts and Sciences, 51st Oscars Highlights: https://www.oscars.org/videos-photos/51st-oscars-highlights/?. Coppola's remarks are part of the clip that culminates in the awarding of Best Picture by John Wayne.

35. For a dissenting view on this, see Hadley Freeman, *Life Moves Pretty Fast: The Lessons We Learned from Eighties Movies* (New York: Simon & Schuster, 2015).

36. The best history of this is Peter Biskind's *Down and Dirty Pictures: Miramax, Sundance, and the Rise of Independent Film* (New York: Simon & Schuster, 2004), which is a sequel of sorts to Biskind, *Easy Riders, Raging Bulls*.

Chapter 4   Starting Over

1. David Sheff, *The Playboy Interviews with John Lennon and Yoko Ono*, ed. G. Barry Golson (New York: The Playboy Press, 1981), 4. This book, a longer

version of the conversations between Sheff and Lennon conducted in September 1980 and published in the magazine, are the closest thing we have to a final testament from Lennon.

2. Robert Palmer, "John Lennon: Must an Artist Self-Destruct?" *New York Times*, November 9, 1980, C15.

3. All references to chart position come from weekly editions of *Billboard* magazine, the standard of the industry. In writing this chapter, I used online data, but repeatedly consulted Joel Whitburn, ed., *The Billboard Book of Top 40 Hits* (New York: Billboard Publications, 1985).

4. Kenneth Womack, *John Lennon 1980: The Last Days in the Life* (London: Omnibus Press, 2020), 14, 61–63. "I got frantic at one point that I was supposed to be *creating* things, so I wrote down about two hundred pages of mad stuff," Lennon told Sheff. "It's there in a box, but it isn't right," (121).

5. Womack, 123–141.

6. Sheff, *The Playboy Interviews*, 155.

7. "Laurie Johnston, Women's Group to Observe Rights Here Today," *New York Times*, August 25, 1972, 40.

8. The interview can be found at http://www.beatlesinterviews.org/db1980.0929.beatles.html, accessed January 25, 2021.

9. Palmer, "Must an Artist Self-Destruct?"

10. Sheff, *The Playboy Interviews*, 187.

11. Michaelangelo Matos, *Can't Slow Down: How 1984 Became Pop's Blockbuster Year* (New York: Hachette, 2020), 3; Recording Industry Association of America database, accessed January 27, 2021, https://www.riaa.com/u-s-sales-database/; Peter Tschmuck, "The Recession in the Music Industry: A Cause Analysis," Music Business Research, March 29, 2010, https://musicbusinessresearch.wordpress.com/2010/03/29/the-recession-in-the-music-industry-a-cause-analysis/#:~:text=Between%201977%20and%201980%2C%20sales,sold%20between%201978%20and%201980.

12. For a good overview of the major pop genres and their relationship to each other in the last half-century, see Kalefa Senneh, *Major Labels: A History of Pop Music in Seven Genres* (New York: Penguin Press, 2021).

13. Much of this analysis draws from Jim Cullen, *A Short History of the Modern Media* (Malden, MA: Wiley Blackwell, 2014), 206.

14. Richard Harrington, "Donna Summer's Saving Grace," *Washington Post*, July 29, 1981, https://www.washingtonpost.com/archive/lifestyle/1981/07/29/donna-summers-saving-grace/196b609d-8caf-417f-aae9-af9789dc8b2b/.

15. Matos, *Can't Slow Down*, 170.

16. This paragraph draws on Cullen, *A Short History of the Modern Media*, 221.

17. Much of the information in this and the ensuing paragraph draws from Cullen, *Short History of the Modern Media*, 207–208.

18. You can actually watch him do this in a bizarre moment in which he calls Denver "my friend," leading Denver to respond, "I don't know what to say," accessed February 1, 2021, https://www.youtube.com/watch?v=Qf3t3unp-Gg.

19. Marissa R. Moss, "Inside Country Music's Polarizing 'Urban Cowboy' Movement," *Rolling Stone*, June 6, 2020, https://www.rollingstone.com/music /music-country/inside-country-musics-polarizing-urban-cowboy-movement-38886/.

20. For more on the Eagles, Ronstadt, and Browne in particular, see Ronald Brownstein, *Rock Me on the Water: 1974—the Year Los Angeles Transformed Movies, Music, Television and Politics* (New York: Harper, 2021).

21. Paul Elliot, "The Inside Story of AC/DC's *Back in Black*, the Bestselling Rock Album of All Time," Guitar World, July 23, 2020, https://www.guitarworld .com/features/the-inside-story-of-acdcs-back-in-black.

22. For a truly marvelous and revealing demonstration of the way a hit song is made, see "Nile Rodgers Tells the Story of 'Let's Dance'": https://www.youtube .com/watch?v=NlDCPCwVNUw.

23. Fred Bronson, *The Billboard Book of #1 Hits* (New York: Billboard Books, 2003), accessed February 4, 2021, https://www.superseventies.com/sw _goodtimes.html.

24. George Simpson, "Another One Bites the Dust 40th Anniversary: How Michael Jackson Influenced the Queen Hit," *UK Express*, August 13, 2020, https://www.express.co.uk/entertainment/music/1322336/Another-One-Bites -The-Dust-40th-anniversary-Michael-Jackson-Queen-bassist-John-Deacon.

25. Fred Schruers, "Bruce Springsteen and the Secret of the World," *Rolling Stone*, February 5, 1981, https://www.rollingstone.com/music/music-news/bruce -springsteen-and-the-secret-of-the-world-178120/.

26. "John Lennon Praises Springsteen's 'Hungry Heart' in Final Interview Hours before His Death," beatleshistorian.com, August 22, 2016, https:// beatleshistorian.com/?p=655; Jonathan Cott, "John Lennon: The Last Interview," *Rolling Stone*, December 23, 2010, https://www.rollingstone.com/feature/john -lennon-the-last-interview-179443/. Cott waited thirty years to release the transcripts of the interview, which he decided not to publish in the immediate aftermath of Lennon's death.

27. Dave Marsh, *Born to Run: The Bruce Springsteen Story* (repr.; New York: Dell, 1981), 256.

28. Jim Cullen, *Born in the USA: Bruce Springsteen and the American Tradition* (New York: HarperCollins, 1997), 177–181.

29. Dave Marsh, *Bruce Springsteen Two Hearts: The Definitive Biography, 1972–2003* (New York: Routledge, 2004), 276.

Chapter 5   Ebb and Flow

1. Andy Meisler, "When J.R. Was Shot the Cliffhanger Was Born," *New York Times*, May 7, 1995, https://www.nytimes.com/1995/05/07/arts/television-when -j-r-was-shot-the-cliffhanger-was-born.html?pagewanted=all. In this chapter, all references to ratings refer to those gauged by the television industry's barometer, the A.C. Nielsen Company. The *Dallas* episode in question lost its status as the most watched TV episode to the *M*A*S*H* finale of 1983. For more details, see Jim Cullen, *From Memory to History: Television Versions of the Twentieth Century* (New Brunswick, NJ: Rutgers University Press, 2021).

2. Hagman recounts this story, and the hoopla surrounding J.R.'s fate, in his 2004 interview with Television Academy, an important video archive of TV history, accessed February 28, 2021, https://interviews.televisionacademy.com /interviews/larry-hagman. Director Lee Rich notes the endings in his interview, accessed March 1, 2021, https://interviews.televisionacademy.com/interviews /lee-rich; the button is mentioned in Rick Perlstein, *Reaganland: America's Right Turn, 1976–80* (New York: Simon & Schuster, 2020), 841.

3. Jacobs described the origins of the show in his Television Academy interview, accessed February 28, 2021, https://interviews.televisionacademy.com /interviews/david-jacobs?clip=63318#interview-clips.

4. Kimberly Potts, "Comfort Viewing: 3 Reasons Why I Love *Dallas*," *New York Times*, December 18, 2020, https://www.nytimes.com/2020/12/18/arts /television/dallas-jr-ewing.html.

5. It was J.R.'s sister-in-law, Kristin. Just as J.R. was about to call the police on her, she told him she was pregnant with his baby. So he did not turn her in, though it was eventually revealed that the child was not actually his, and Kristin, who became a drug addict, died in a fall. Her child was adopted by Pam and Bobby, his story to be carried into the second iteration of the series between 2012 and 2015.

6. Alex Madrigal, "When Did TV Watching Peak?" *The Atlantic*, May 30, 2018, https://www.theatlantic.com/technology/archive/2018/05/when-did-tv -watching-peak/561464/.

7. "The Man with the Golden Gut: Fred Silverman Has Made ABC Number 1," *Time*, September 5, 1977, http://content.time.com/time/subscriber/article /0,33009,915399,00.html.

8. For more on *M*A*S*H* and its ratings performance, see the chapter on the show in Cullen, *From Memory to History: Television Versions of the Twentieth Century*.

9. Doug Hill and Jeff Weingrad, *Saturday Night: A Backstage History of Saturday Night Live* (New York: Beech Tree Books, 1986), 430–440; Tom Shales

and James Andrew Miller, *Live from New York: An Uncensored History of* Saturday Night Live (New York: Little, Brown, 2002), 201–204.

10. Aaron Spelling, *A Prime-Time Life* (New York: St. Martin's Press, 1996), 110.

11. See, for example, the gag reels with outtakes from the show, accessed March 5, 2021, https://www.youtube.com/watch?v=e750Hr2OEB4.

12. The information in this paragraph draws from Jim Cullen, *Democratic Empire: The United States since 1945* (Malden, MA: Wiley Blackwell, 2017), 168.

13. Emily Todd VanDerWerff, "*Happy Days* Became One of the Biggest Hits on TV by Selling Its Soul," AV Club, August 27, 2012, https://tv.avclub.com /happy-days-became-one-of-the-biggest-hits-on-tv-by-sell-1798233067.

14. Fred Fox Jr., "In Defense of *Happy Days*'s 'Jump the Shark' Episode," *Los Angeles Times*, September 3, 2010, https://www.latimes.com/archives/la-xpm -2010-sep-03-la-et-jump-the-shark-20100903-story.html.

15. You can see it for yourself: https://www.youtube.com/watch?v =HLTx5ZwJiSo (accessed March 6, 2021).

16. For more on the history of CNN, see Lisa Napoli, *Up All Night: Ted Turner, CNN, and the Birth of 24-Hour News* (New York: Abrams Press, 2020).

17. Jane Hall, "CBS News Suspends Rooney for Remarks about Blacks," *Los Angeles Times*, February 9, 1990, https://www.latimes.com/archives/la-xpm-1990 -02-09-mn-236-story.html.

18. A list of *60 Minutes* stories can be found at https://danratherjournalist.org /investigative-journalist/60-minutes/60-minutes-additional-materials /document-list-60-minutes-shows, accessed March 7, 2021.

19. See Ira Rosen, *Ticking Clock, Behind the Scenes at 60 Minutes* (New York: St. Martin's Press, 2021), 2021.

20. David Bauder, "*60 Minutes* Tops Television Ratings with Coronavirus Report," Associated Press, March 11, 2020, https://apnews.com/article/ee95c14e 0d32f31baa160d639bac491b.

21. Stephen Hamilton, "Best Guest Stars on *The Love Boat*," ca. 2016, accessed March 7, 2021, https://vocal.media/geeks/best-guest-stars-on-the -love-boat.

22. "Richard Simmons" on *Real People*: https://www.youtube.com/watch?v =frFqM8tINtI (March 7, 2021).

23. See the hang-gliding dog clip, accessed March 7, 2020, https://www .youtube.com/watch?v=iGc4QTA1enk&list=PLrnUF7vIL1AcUQDKdg _9sGpDnr6SQM5fH&index=23; Ken Kelly, "Forty Years Ago: That's Incredible Aired Pre-Jackass TV Stunts," VCR Movies and Culture, March 3, 2020, https:// ultimateclassicrock.com/thats-incredible-tv-show/.

24. For more on Rushing's background, see *The Real Duke of Hazzard: The Jerry Rushing Story* (Lake Mary, FL: Creation House, 2005).

25. Christopher Hoitash, "'Boss Hogg' Sorrell Booke Was a Counter-Intelligence Agent in the Korean War," War History Online, November 11, 2018, https://www.warhistoryonline.com/instant-articles/boss-hogg-sorrell-booke.html.

26. Frank Pallotta, "*Dukes of Hazzard* Episodes Pulled from TV Land," CNN Money, July 3, 2015, https://money.cnn.com/2015/07/01/media/dukes-of-hazzard-tv-land/index.html.

27. This was something the author discovered in a lively Facebook exchange with friends from all walks of life.

Chapter 6   Turning the Page

1. Angus Burgin, "Age of Certainty: Galbraith, Friedman, and the Public Life of Economic Ideas," *History of Political Economy*, 45 (annual supplement 2013): 199; Bernard D. Nossiter, "Galbraith and the BBC: Entertaining Economics," *Washington Post*, January 8, 1977, https://www.washingtonpost.com/archive/lifestyle/1977/01/08/galbraith-and-the-bbc-economics-that-entertain/50fc2648-0c77-4bae-a859-36d2784427cc/; John J. O'Connor, "TV: Galbraith Offers 'A Personal View,'" *New York Times*, May 19, 1977, https://www.nytimes.com/1977/05/19/archives/tv-galbraith-offers-a-personal-view.html.

2. Burgin, "Age of Certainty," 193, 204–205.

3. William McGurn, "The Man Who Made Milton Friedman a Star," *Wall Street Journal*, October 30, 2020, https://www.wsj.com/articles/the-man-who-made-milton-friedman-a-star-11604073953.

4. *Free to Choose* is widely available on Amazon.com and other platforms; the two clips in question can be seen at https://www.youtube.com/watch?v=26QxO49Ycxo; and https://www.youtube.com/watch?v=U6vrteO-6xw, respectively, accessed April 11, 2021.

5. McGurn, "The Man Who Made."

6. Milton Friedman and Rose Friedman, *Free to Choose: A Personal Statement* (1980; New York: Harcourt, 1990), 11, 148.

7. Friedman and Friedman, 137, 226.

8. McGurn, "The Man Who Made."

9. Burgin, "Age of Certainty," 213.

10. Stephen King, *Firestarter* (1980; New York: Pocket Books, 2016), 564.

11. Elaine Woo, "Marilyn French Dies at 79: Author of the Feminist Classic *The Women's Room*," *Los Angeles Times*, May 5, 2009, https://www.latimes.com/local/obituaries/la-me-marilyn-french5-2009may05-story.html.

12. "A Record $3.2 Million Is Pledged by Bantam for New Krantz Novel," *New York Times*, September 14, 1979, https://www.nytimes.com/1979/09/14/archives/a-record-32-million-is-pledged-by-bantam-for-new-krantz-novel-in.html.

13. Judith Krantz, *Princess Daisy* (1980; New York: Bantam Books, 1992), 24, 267.

14. Krantz, 227, 341, 388.

15. Margalit Fox, "Sidney Sheldon, Author of Steamy Novels, Dies at 89," *New York Times*, February 1, 2007, https://www.nytimes.com/2007/02/01 /obituaries/01sheldon.html?ex=1185944400&en=6926e71f21afa7d5&ei =5087&excamp=GGGNsidneysheldon; Bob Thomas, "Author Sidney Sheldon Dies at 89," Associated Press, accessed April 20, 2021, http://bachlab.balbach.net /coolreading/SidneySheldon.txt. The *Times* obituary cites the 300 million figure, which is also featured on the back cover of the most recent edition of Sidney Sheldon, *Rage of Angels* (New York: Grand Central Publishing, 2017).

16. Ken Follett, *The Key to Rebecca* (1980; New York: New American Library, 1985), 170.

17. Nancy Friday, *My Secret Garden: Women's Sexual Fantasies* (1973; New York: RosettaBooks, 2013 [e-book]), introduction; Nancy Friday, *Men in Love, Men's Sexual Fantasies: The Triumph of Love Over Rage* (1980; New York: Delta, 1998); Anita Gates, "Nancy Friday, 84, Best-Selling Student of Gender Politics, Dies," *New York Times*, November 5, 2017, https://www.nytimes.com/2017/11/05 /obituaries/nancy-friday-84-best-selling-student-of-gender-politics-dies.html.

18. Gay Talese, *Thy Neighbor's Wife* (1980; New York: Ecco, 2009), 491–495.

19. Talese, 192, 287.

20. Talese, 551–553.

21. Casey quoted in Nick Foster, "Projects Draw Attention to Argentine Countryside," *New York Times*, February 26, 2010, https://www.nytimes.com /2010/02/26/greathomesanddestinations/26iht-reargen.html.

22. Dave Itzkoff, "Fox Plans New *Cosmos*, with Seth McFarlane as Producer," *New York Times*, August 5, 2011, https://www.nytimes.com/2011/08/05/arts /television/fox-plans-new-cosmos-with-seth-macfarlane-as-a-producer.html; Carl Sagan, *Cosmos* (1980; New York: Ballentine, 1985). The cover of this edition boasts the book has sold 5 million copies, and that was four decades ago.

23. David Marchese, "Neil deGrasse Tyson Thinks Science Can Reign Supreme Again," *New York Times Magazine*, April 19, 2021, https://www.nytimes .com/interactive/2021/04/19/magazine/neil-degrasse-tyson-interview.html.

24. Birnbach recounted the origins of the project in a February 2021 podcast ACL (A Continuous Lean), https://www.acl.news/p/prep. For a contemporary description of how the book came about, see Linda Leher, "The World According to Prep: A Book Becomes a Media Event," *Brown Alumni Monthly*, April 1981, https://archive.org/details/brownalumnimonth817brow/page/36/mode/2up. See also Dudley Clendinen, "Behind the Bestsellers: The Preppy Handbook," *New York Times*, January 4, 1981.

25. Leher, "The World According to Prep," 38; ACL podcast, February 2021, https://www.acl.news/p/prep; Lisa Birnbach, ed., *The Preppy Handbook* (New York: Workman Publishing, 1980), 11.

26. Birnbach, *The Preppy Handbook*, 35, 32.

27. Birnbach, 69, 86, 61, 157.

Chapter 7   Inflection Point

1. The phrase has been attributed to longtime Democratic "Wise Man" Clark Clifford, who used it in a conversation in September 1980. See Arnold Sawislak, "Reagan Called 'Amiable Dunce' on New Washington Tape," United Press International archive, October 10, 1981, https://www.upi.com/Archives/1981/10/10/Reagan-called-amiable-dunce-on-new-Washington-tape/3026371534400/.

2. Adam Clymer, "Post Convention Polls: Quick Turnabout, as Usual," *New York Times*, August 20, 1980, 1.

3. Rick Perlstein, *Reaganland: America's Right Turn, 1976–1980* (New York: Simon & Schuster, 2020), 838–839, 841–846.

4. William Lunch, "Shadows of '64 and '72," *New York Times*, September 9, 1980, A19.

5. James David Barber, *The Presidential Character: Predicting Performance in the White House* (1972; New York: Routledge, 2019); James David Barber, "Worrying about Reagan," *New York Times*, September 8, 1980, A19; Reagan quoted in James T. Patterson, *Restless Giant: The United States from Watergate to Bush v. Gore* (New York: Oxford University Press, 2005), 160.

6. Perlstein, *Reaganland*, 849.

7. Perlstein, 856–859.

8. Patterson, *Restless Giant*, 147.

9. Adam Clymer, "Reagan Viewed in Poll as Leader; Carter Cited on Concern for Poor," *New York Times*, September 17, 1980, A1; Hedrick Smith, "Reagan Given Edge in 'Big 9' Battleground States," *New York Times*, September 13, 1980, A32, Hedrick Smith, "With Month to Go, Reagan Is Given Lead in Electoral Vote," *New York Times*, October 5, 1980, A1.

10. David A. Graham, "The Myth of Gerald Ford's Fatal 'Soviet Domination' Gaffe," *The Atlantic*, August 2, 2016, https://www.theatlantic.com/politics/archive/2016/08/the-myth-of-gerald-fords-disastrous-soviet-domination-gaffe/493958/.

11. Edward Walsh (with Lou Cannon), "Carter Bars Debate with Anderson," *Washington Post*, May 28, 1980, https://web.archive.org/web/20201006082615if_/https://www.washingtonpost.com/archive/politics/1980/05/28/carter-bars-debate-with-anderson/c5b49650-d3dc-43e8-b646-60c421bbd8de/.

12. The cartoon was reprinted in the *New York Times* on October 12, page E4.

13. Perlstein, *Reaganland*, 876; Leslie Bennetts, "NOW Rejects All Three for President, Calls Reagan 'Medieval,'" *New York Times*, October 6, 1980, A20; Douglas Kneeland, "Reagan Pledges Woman on Court," *New York Times*, October 15, 1980, A1; Hedrick Smith, "Poll Shows the President Has Pulled Even with Reagan, *New York Times*, October 23, 1980, A1.

14. Perlstein, *Reaganland*, 898.

15. For one set of comprehensive coverage of the debate, see the package of stories beginning on page A1 of the *New York Times* on October 29, 1980. Perlstein zeroes in on the Medicare/Medicaid exchange in *Reaganland*, 899–901. You can see it yourself at https://www.youtube.com/watch?v=qN7gDRjTNf4. On the origins of "teflon president," see the entry in Taegan Goddard's Political Dictionary website, accessed May 20, 2021, https://politicaldictionary.com/words/teflon-president/. For one example of the ad the Reagan team ran, see the *New York Times*, November 5, 1980, B9.

16. Patterson, *Restless Giant*, 148; Adam Clymer, "Polls Show Reagan and Carter Nearly Even in Last Polls," *New York Times*, November 3, 1980, A1.

17. At the time and long after, there were suspicions that the Reagan camp was illegally in contact with the Iranian government and trying to make a deal to delay the release of the hostages. This case was made most systematically by National Security Adviser Gary Sick in *October Surprise: America's Hostages in Iran and the Election of Ronald Reagan* (New York: Random House, 1992). However, key details in Sick's argument have been contested or disproved, and a House of Representatives investigation in 1993 found no evidence of wrongdoing. It may be that something happened—Reagan adviser William Casey, who went on to run the CIA, would appear to have few compunctions about such schemes, as suggested by his role in the Iran-Contra affair—but at this point the Reagan operation is generally presumed innocent.

18. Perlstein, *Reaganland*, 902–905.

19. Perlstein cites a figure of 52.4 percent; Patterson 54.7, a shade lower than the 54.8 percent of 1976, another low turnout year.

20. Data taken from the American Presidency Project, University of California at Santa Barbara, accessed May 2, 2021, https://www.presidency.ucsb.edu/statistics/elections/1980.

21. Patterson, *Restless Giant*, 149.

22. Perlstein, *Reaganland*, 909; Thomas B. Edsall and Mary D. Edsall, *Chain Reaction: The Impact of Race, Rights and Taxes on American Politics* (New York: W.W. Norton, 1991).

23. Adam Clymer, "Poll Shows Iran and Economy Hurt Carter among Late-Shifting Voters," *New York Times*, November 6, 1980, A1; Perlstein, *Reaganland*, 909–911.

24. Harold Jackson, "Aides Tell a Tearful Carter 'It's All Over,'" *The Guardian*, November 5, 1980, https://www.theguardian.com/world/1980/nov/05/usa.alexbrummer1; Carter's speech can be seen on C-Span, accessed May 2, 2021, https://www.c-span.org/video/?418299-1/president-jimmy-carter-concession-speech.

Conclusion

1. Jim Cullen, *Imperfect Presidents: Tales of Misadventure and Triumph* (New York: Palgrave, 2007), 39.

2. Haynes Johnson, *Sleepwalking through History: America in the Reagan Years* (New York: Norton, 1991), 19–21; Leslie Bennetts, "With a New First Lady, a New Style," *New York Times*, January 21, 1981, B6.

3. Pete Early, "National Pride Unites Throng of Revelers at Inauguration," *Washington Post*, January 21, 1981, https://www.washingtonpost.com/archive/politics/1981/01/21/national-pride-unites-throng-of-revelers-at-inauguration/848d05c4-b921-4912-b947-d81e1d1124ff/.

4. The text of Reagan's speech is available at Yale University's Avalon Project, https://avalon.law.yale.edu/20th_century/reagan1.asp; Richard Hollaran, "The Pledge of Private Treptow," *New York Times*, January 21, 1981, https://www.nytimes.com/1981/01/21/us/the-pledge-of-private-treptow.html.

5. Johnson, *Sleepwalking*, 24–25, 39; John Kifner, "Tehran Captors Call Out Insults as the 52 Leave," *New York Times*, January 21, 1981, A1.

6. Lynn Rosselini, "'Honey, I forgot to Duck,' Injured Reagan Tells Wife," *New York Times*, March 31, 1981, https://www.nytimes.com/1981/03/31/us/honey-i-forgot-to-duck-injured-reagan-tells-wife.html.

7. Robert Sherrill, "Looking at America," *New York Times*, September 14, 1980, https://archive.nytimes.com/www.nytimes.com/books/99/09/26/specials/terkel-dreams.html. Studs Terkel, *American Dreams: Lost and Found* (1980; New York: The New Press, 2005), 405, 38.

8. Terkel, 19.

INDEX

Numbers in italics indicate figures

ABOUT THE AUTHOR

JIM CULLEN teaches history at the recently founded upper division of Greenwich Country Day School in Greenwich, Connecticut. He is the author of numerous books, among them *The American Dream: A Short History of an Idea That Shaped a Nation*; *Those Were the Days: Why* All in the Family *Still Matters*; and *Best Class You Never Had: A Novel*. His essays and reviews have appeared in the *Washington Post*, CNN.com, *USA Today, Rolling Stone*, and the *American Historical Review*, among other publications. A father of four, Jim lives in Hastings-on-Hudson, New York, with his wife, Lyde Cullen Sizer, Dean of the College at Sarah Lawrence College.